Advance Praise for *The Blueprint*

"Jim Fannin guided the overall mindset transformation of our company from top to bottom. His blueprint and concrete S.C.O.R.E.® tools helped propel our bank to tenfold growth and record profits, as well as create an atmosphere of work–life balance."

–**Julie McAllister**, mother, wife, and business executive

"I had mentally quit on myself. However, within 30 days, Jim Fannin's blueprint for successful living took hold as I booked my first ever acting job. Now, years later I'm the star in a one-person Off-Broadway play. There is no ceiling or limit to my success, and Jim not only helped me to see that, but set me into motion."

–**Courtney Abbiatti**, Screen & Stage Actress

"Jim helped design my life Blueprint when I was a student athlete at Notre Dame and it has been manifested to perfection with his tools and techniques. I was drafted by the New York Yankees. Now with a .380 batting average in my first year in the minors, my "Next" challenge is my only thought."

–**Ryan Lidge**, New York Yankees

"Jim Fannin has coached seven players into the world's top ten. I know! I was one of them. In addition, he helped me win four Wimbledon Doubles titles. After 40 years I still use his tools and techniques. Pretty amazing."

–**Peter Fleming**, four-time Wimbledon Doubles Champion

"Reaching the Hall of Fame...I mean, I owe it to Jim Fannin. To be honest, he taught me to live in the Zone. Once I started using Jim's S.C.O.R.E.® System and following The Blueprint, it changed my entire life and career. Check it out. It will change your life forever."

–**Frank Thomas**, MLB All-Star; MVP; Hall of Fame

"As a corporate growth architect for many of the world's leading organizations, I design, develop, and deliver strategies grounded in a sound blueprint. I used The Blueprint to architect a life strategy for myself, while also applying the tools to my business and the businesses I serve."

–**Drew Boston**, CEO, Moxi, LLC

"Simultaneously launching my consulting company, not-for-profit foundation, and media career plus completing my first mainstream book are all daunting tasks. Jim Fannin's Blueprint and tools are turning them *all* into reality."

–**Dr. Sweta Chakraborty**, Cognitive Behavioral Scientist & Risk Expert

"As my executive coach, Jim Fannin taught lessons with his proprietary S.C.O.R.E.® tools that will last a lifetime. He gets swift and enduring results."

–**Mark Vachon**, former President & CEO of GE Healthcare Americas

"I've conducted over 50 Golf in the Zone™ Schools alongside Jim Fannin. I've learned something new every time. It's been truly amazing."

–**Brian Mogg**, Golf Digest Top 50; Golf Magazine Top 100 Instructors

"After a two-day Jim Fannin retreat, our team bonded like never before and the results were immediately measureable. Over 10 years later I still use his Blueprint and tools."

–**Steve Patscott**, GE Healthcare

"Jim Fannin's Blueprint, with its concrete tools and techniques, has helped me overcome a serious medical challenge, as well as simplify and balance my personal and professional life."

–**Kevin Gates**, President & CEO, Veterans First Mortgage

"I have been doing golf schools and corporate outings with Jim Fannin and have seen some amazing things occur. Not only does Jim make a lasting change in the students' golf games, but also, he makes a lasting change in their lives. I have seen him restore marriages, revive careers, and lower handicaps. He has enriched my life. I've seen him change others. I know he can change you. Your golf handicap is just the beginning."

–**Mike Adams**, Golf Digest Top 50 Instructor; Golf Magazine Top 100

"As a television and print journalist, businesswoman, and mother of two, I find Jim Fannin's tools simple and adaptable for use in all facets of life. It works! And it's the best gift you can share with others"

–**Mary Laney**, Emmy Award-winning TV Anchorwoman and Print Journalist

"I was with Jim my entire career. He helped me become an All-Star. Hitting four home runs in one game was an amazing Zone experience that I'll never forget."

–**Mike Cameron**, former MLB All-Star

"Having spent 28 years in athletic administration, I was always searching for the answer to the question, 'How can you help athletes perform at a higher level?' Jim Fannin and his S.C.O.R.E.® System give you the Blueprint and tools to get your team in the Zone and reach peak performance."

–**Dr. John Planek**, Lewis University Athletic Director

"For over 15 years, I've used Jim Fannin's concrete tools both professionally and personally. They have worked with my son, daughter, golf game, and business with great success. All are thriving. I am truly grateful."

–**Gus Sylvan**, State Farm Agent, Columbia, SC

"The investment made in Jim's Blueprint and tools has been returned 20 to 1 for our Toyota dealership."

–**George Collins**, General Manager, Miami, FL

"Jim Fannin's S.C.O.R.E.® blueprint, tools and techniques work! It is the secret formula for thinking like a champion and performing in the Zone."

–**Scott Mitchell**, Former All-Pro NFL Quarterback

"Jim's Blueprint with its tools and techniques helped take my already successful business to another amazing level. In addition, his guidance helped my overall relationship with my family. It's brought great peace of mind to be the best person I can be to the people who matter most in my life and my work."

–**Lou Cassara**, CLU, ChFC, Leading Financial Advisor

"In my 24 years in this business, I have seen many incredible speakers, including John Wooden! All have been inspiring and all have been privileged experiences to me. None have made such a profound change in me personally as Jim Fannin."

–**Linda Fulgenzi**, Merrill Lynch

"I was the Director of Jim Fannin's highly successful S.C.O.R.E.® Tennis Academy for 16 years. His S.C.O.R.E.® Success System helped hundreds of junior tennis players play college tennis, resulting in over $24 million in scholarships. In addition, we coached seven national amateur champions and dozens of state high school champions. What a legacy!"

–**Rick Goldwasser**, Tennis Professional, Flagstaff, AZ

"After spending time with Jim Fannin each person on my team left with a customized life blueprint with concrete tools. If you haven't had a seminar with Jim, your employees are missing out."

–**Jerry Richards**, Regional Manager, Waddell & Reed

"Jim has helped me as a player, coach, and teacher. His S.C.O.R.E.® System continues to pay dividends."

–**Maggie Will**, 3-time LPGA winner

"Until I started working with Jim Fannin, I had moderate success in my voice-over career. Once I created a Blueprint and applied his tools and techniques, my business underwent a positive fundamental shift. Jim understands what it takes to get the most out of life and business, if you apply what he teaches. I applied it and I'm enjoying tremendous results."

–**Lee Crooks**, Voice-over Professional, Milwaukee, WI

THE
BLUEPRINT

THE
BLUEPRINT

A PROVEN PLAN FOR
SUCCESSFUL LIVING

JIM FANNIN
AMERICA'S ZONECOACH®

A SAVIO REPUBLIC BOOK
An Imprint of Post Hill Press

The Blueprint:
A Proven Plan for Successful Living
© 2018 by Jim Fannin
All Rights Reserved

ISBN: 978-1-68261-631-4
ISBN (eBook): 978-1-68261-632-1

Cover Design by Soren Thielemann, eatdanish.com
Interior Design and Composition by Greg Johnson/Textbook Perfect

posthillpress.com
New York • Nashville
Published in the United States of America

Jim Fannin Brands, Inc. offers books, e-Books, audio CDs, video, e-Courses, executive coaching, life coaching, sports coaching, seminars, keynotes, retreats, and other properties that may be purchased for life, business, and sports from jimfannin.com.

The S.C.O.R.E.® Success System, ZoneCoach®, 90-Second Rule™, Go To Higher Ground™ and other tools referenced in this book are federally registered marks and are the sole property of Jim Fannin Brands, Inc.

*They say "It takes a village to raise a child," and from its inception to final maturity, **The Blueprint** had the stories that contained the visions, dreams, and goals of over 2,000 personal Jim Fannin clients. From forty-plus years of chasing success and being their genuine, authentic best self, it was these clients that created the essence of this book. Thank you.*

Table of Contents

Introduction

Life is complicated. It can be unfair. Living, working, and playing in today's culture of economic uncertainty, political divisiveness, and social unrest has complex challenges.

"Less is more" may seem like a pipedream, because thriving today has even more obstacles and impediments. The world is more difficult and chaotic than ever. Competition for love, money, market share, social status, ranking, power, freedom, and independence is ferocious and inexorable.

Every day you are bombarded by half-truths and lies about what's best for you:

- "Studies show that eating a whole food, plant-based diet is ideal."
- "Studies show that eating as our ancestral hunter-gatherers ate is ideal."
- "Ab exercises will get you better abs."
- "Low fat!"
- "High fat!"
- "No pain. No gain."

This can easily lead to confusion. Dialogue in America today is sprinkled with discord, mistrust, and negativity. Misinformation is rampant. The human race has never had more information so swiftly inundating our collective minds from social media, traditional, and Internet news outlets, friends, family, team members, and co-workers. Too much information can be overwhelming.

Overthinking is rampant. Underachievement is real.

At the same time, the world's attention span is shrinking. We spend more time in the past and future than living in the moment. According to research firm **Dscout**, "The typical cellphone user touches his or her phone 2,617 times every day with extreme users (top ten percent) touching their phones more than 5,400 times daily." The research found that "average users spend 145 minutes on their phones and engage in seventy-six phone sessions per day." Yes...we are addicted to our mobile devices.

But even though we are connected to the outside world, we seldom look each other in the eye long enough to discern eye color. We rarely dine as a family, unless it's a special occasion. Daily bickering is commonplace. Video games rule as a distraction to what's happening in the real world. Daily personal dialogue is more about what we don't want than what we do want. Self-discipline, concentration, optimism, relaxation, and enjoyment change by the hour and are even missing at some points of the day. Focus is easily disturbed.

As a whole, we are more depressed, dissatisfied, angry, unhappy, confused, impatient, pissed off, disgruntled, lonely, dejected, and disappointed than ever. We long for simplicity. We covet life balance, but do not know how to achieve it. We are ready to be our genuine, authentic best selves, but are stymied by too many unproven options, or none at all. "Tell me what to do" is what we seek from authorities and experts. Finding these people usually takes trial and error and the damage and wasted time is usually too expensive in time, energy, and money.

Some of us have even *settled*. These are real quotes that I've heard.

▶ "My relationship is okay. I love her. We're both tired. We are intimate, but not as often as before. I can manage."
▶ "I know my kids are doing things they shouldn't be doing. I'm tired of tracking their every move. They'll be okay. We'll figure it out."
▶ "My job's not the best, but it's a job. I'll eventually find the right place for me."
▶ "I want to be a writer so badly. I know my novel will sell. I'll get to it sooner or later."

▶ "I've gotten so fat, I need new clothes. I need a diet and a trainer. I'll start next week after I dine at my favorite restaurant. LOL."

▶ "I love my wife. I love my kids. I make $850K per year, own three cars and have a summer home in the Hamptons. Yet, I'm so miserable and don't know why."

Fortunately, there are people that still believe in themselves. This is where you come in. You believe in yourself, but wonder why you haven't achieved everything you've dreamed. You wish you had a sense of expectancy—a sense of KNOWING that you can and will accomplish something great. You may know what you want, but are unsure about any or all of the *who, what, when, where, why,* and *how* answers that will lead you to fulfilling your dreams or visions. Is this you?

You know you can have a better life. You know you're talented. You know you're as smart as the next person (if not smarter) in your field of endeavor. You know your best days are ahead of you. You just need an edge in your pocket. As one client told me in confidence,

"I long for a plan that ensures my efforts manifest into a life my parents would be most proud."

If you answer **"YES"** to one or more of these questions, you'll find the **"HOW"** in this book. Do you:

▶ Want more in life with less thought?
▶ Want peak performance? Want to attract the Zone?
▶ Want only positive, rewarding days?
▶ Want dynamic relationships at work, school, and home?
▶ Want to be your authentic, genuine, best self?
▶ Want wellness and longevity?
▶ Want a proven, simple plan with a compass for staying on course?

At the moment of your conception, your DNA created a blueprint for your growth. Your height, your eye color, your race, and your biological sex were all put onto a blueprint that guided your physical growth.

This blueprint isn't only for your body, though. Your mind also has a blueprint, one that gives you your talent and desires—the qualities that make you uniquely *you*.

For successful people, even though the parts of the blueprint may have been added to, edited, or deleted along the way, the overall blueprint remained intact until the mission was accomplished.

Just as all buildings, homes, roads, bridges, and entire communities have a blueprint that illuminates a pathway to completion, humans also need a blueprint for developing a life of simplicity, balance, and abundance.

Successful humans need a blueprint.

The Blueprint draws from my experiences, proprietary research, client interaction, and a thirsty quest for each human to evolve into his or her genuine, authentic, best self.

Welcome to my life's work of more than 40 years. All of my thousands of clients have been on-boarded in the same way. The following is one of my typical ways to challenge a new client as he or she is introduced to a new way of thinking and living.

Here are four questions I've asked new clients and thousands of champions during my career. As you embark on a new chapter in your life, how will you answer them?

"What is success for you?" This has stumped most people. All knew what they *didn't* want. Most did NOT have specific answers fleshed out. Each needed a blueprint, since none of my more than 2,000 clients arrived with one tucked under their arms. With few exceptions, the ones that answered this question often sold themselves short.

"What do you want to accomplish and when?" Most knew what they wanted to accomplish, but didn't know how or when to consistently organize the execution.

"What challenges keep you from success?" The challenge list has been vast. Most challenges centered on each person's thought process and this had a direct impact on their performance and results. Finding simplicity and life balance was a definite challenge for most clients.

"Would you invest less than three percent of your waking hours to be the best you can be?" Men, women, and children around the world have responded with a resounding "YES." "But how do I do that?" has been their follow-up question.

Four Seekers

To understand the importance of a blueprint, let's look at four peak performers-to-be; all arrived at my door seeking to learn how to consistently attract the "purposeful calm" Zone mindset, where records are broken and dreams come true. All were in quest of answers to their challenges. All sought positive change.

There was a **baseball professional**, a standout **college golfer**, a promising **Internet entrepreneur,** and a renowned **financial advisor.** Although each was vastly different in nationality, age, economic background, and experience, all had one thought in common.

"Be my genuine, authentic, best self."

The **baseball professional** sought consistency: "My performances fluctuate wildly. Sometimes I play well and other times I'm performing nowhere near my potential," he complained. "I know I'm getting in my own way."

The **college golfer** felt the same about her performances: "I seem to overthink during every tournament round," she exclaimed. "When I need to make a putt, I can feel my lack of trust. In addition, my father believes I'm wasting my talent. He puts pressure on me daily and seldom has a positive thing to say to me. Now, I tell him little and he feels we are not as close. He's right! We're not as close and that bothers me even more than my golf game."

The **Internet entrepreneur** was low on confidence and relaxation. He said, "My daily life is out of balance and my professional life is not reflecting peak performance. I am lost in way too many thoughts. In fact, I am having trouble sleeping at night and the stress has reached the boiling point. When something goes wrong in business, I'm taking it out on my family by brooding, being irritable over small things that don't really matter, and intentionally being absent from family functions. I definitely need to change."

Finally, the **financial advisor** felt his prospecting efforts were subpar and he wanted to achieve a higher level of client and overall results. "My client list needs an upgrade!" he said. "I should be making more money with less effort."

These new clients arrived knowing what they didn't want in their lives, business, or sport. All wanted immediate answers to maximizing their talent, experience, and passion. Simplicity and balance were not on their immediate radar, but each coveted these life attributes nevertheless. "I'm tired of mediocrity, especially with my talent level," was a recurring theme. They were done with losing and not realizing their full potential. In fact, they were tired of hearing others even talking about his or her own potential.

Privately, my new clients told me their individual, desired direction. After pushing and prodding from me, each of their visions of where they wanted to go ramped up at least twenty-five percent.

The **baseball professional** knew what he wanted, but needed to get out of his comfort zone in order to compete with the best. Elevating his goals got him fired up. "I can do this process," he told me. "I am an elite player and I understand the Zone," he remarked with a grin. His relaxation has also drastically improved, especially during "moments of truth" when his next pitch dictates the result.

The **college golfer** hadn't thought about the LPGA Tour as college golf was tough enough. This newfound dream started to wake her up and tuck her in bed at night. "I can envision being on tour and I look forward to this next chapter of my life," she stated with optimism. Becoming a professional golfer is possible with her skillset and the thought of financial independence is "both exhilarating and scary." She has taken charge of her father-daughter relationship and Dad has changed his negative ways because of his only child's newfound confidence.

The **Internet entrepreneur** was trying to be all things to all people and this approach wasn't working out. Finally, he settled on two areas of expertise. It was here that he committed to becoming a world-class expert. "I am relieved!" he said. "By honing my skills and narrowing my focus, I now feel confident my clients will get my best. My renewed energy has created a demand and with a simple blueprint, I foresee happy clients and an increased income. As a bonus, the tools and techniques I learned have changed my life at home. A sanctuary of peace and harmony has emerged."

The vision of the **financial advisor** was elevated three hundred percent. "That's a big number!" he exclaimed out loud, as his mind left its comfort zone. This excited and frightened him simultaneously. He has even reignited the romance in his seventeen-year marriage. "This was unexpected and greatly appreciated," rejoiced the happy husband.

Each client's vision and goals are now measurable and attainable. They do the work. I deliver the how.

A personalized master blueprint was designed for each to follow. This included an illuminated pathway for each of the various sections (parenting, finance, career, wellness, relationships, and so forth) of their life. This part of the process had them pleasantly surprised. A customized, master life blueprint was about to provide clarity and, with decisiveness, it would release them from the shackles of the past and the pre-set limitations of the future.

Next, each was provided with **a proven compass.** It was the simple S.C.O.R.E.® Success System with its myriad collection of concrete, proven 90-Second Rule™ tools. With this swift and accurate self-awareness system, staying the course would become much easier. No longer will they get lost in the chaos and complexity of daily living. And if they do get off track, they have simple and easily applicable tools to swiftly adjust, adapt and find their way back to their visions and goals.

Finally, these champions **applied what they learned.** The application of S.C.O.R.E.® and its collection of 90-Second Rule™ tools will take less than three percent of their waking hours. They will all become more focused and have at least twenty-five percent fewer negative or obstructive thoughts. No longer will they stand in their own way. Fear and worry will be things of the past, since they will be swiftly eliminated. No longer will they have to offer excuses. Their personal inner dialogue will be transformed into a new language of positivity. No longer will the victim or judge in them rear its ugly head to sabotage their performances. Their new motto is...

Good fortune favors the bold!

For my new clients, doubt was turned into possibility. Negative stress (if it arrives in the future) can now be vanquished within ninety seconds. Focus was repurposed and strengthened. Confidence was restored and elevated. Self-discipline is now a friend instead of a chore. Passion was rekindled. And it's just the first month for these new life, business, and sports champions!

This is what *The Blueprint: A Proven Plan for Successful Living* is all about. It's not meant to motivate. It simply provides answers and solutions to your current challenges and it provides clarity and assuredness for reaching and or exceeding your life dreams. If this is what you want, then I'm ready to be your coach, mentor, and guide.

Please enjoy *The Blueprint*. Putting it to print was a labor of love. More importantly, get busy and make it part of your life. I look forward to hearing about your results and accomplishments while you become your genuine, authentic best self.

Be in the Zone!

Jim

PART 1

What Life Do You Want to Build?

**There's only one rule to building a successful life,
and it is...there are NO rules.**

CHAPTER 1

How Dreams Come True

When I was a little boy growing up in the Appalachian mountains of eastern Kentucky, my wise grandfather "Pap-paw" whispered to me, "Just 'cause the bushes don't move, don't mean nothing's in there. Jimmy, your dreams are like this."

I replied, "I don't understand..."

"You will!" he stated firmly, as he looked me in the eye long enough to discern eye color.

When Pap-paw and I walked alone in the woods a few miles outside of Hazard, Kentucky, he taught me how to dream. That was our time together. He dreamed of catching fish at the lake.

"Jimmy, I'm going to catch the world's largest fish. It's going to be this big," he laughed as he held both hands as far apart as possible.

I dreamed of an in-ground swimming pool. "Pap-paw, I'm going to have the biggest swimming pool and all my friends will come over and swim with me!" I gleefully exclaimed.

Our dreams would get big and bold. His outlandish, vivid fantasies always made me laugh. "My lake is going to be stocked with the largest bass. When I snap my fingers, they will jump out of the water at my command" and these words instantly triggered my imagination to envision fish leaping above the water in a synchronized swimming maneuver. We both laughed out loud.

Pap-paw and I dreamed about a lot of things. This is the gist of what he told me during our walks in the woods:

"The woods are alive. Know this. They are always alive. Even though you can't see movement, things are happening all around you. Behind the trees, rocks, and bushes, a lot is going on," he said with bright-eyed wonder.

"Just 'cause the bushes don't move, don't mean nothing's in there."

He lowered his voice and whispered, "This is especially true at night when you're asleep. The woods are really active at dark." This thought always put a scare in me.

"Jimmy, your dreams are like the woods. They are alive. A dream is when one single thought is pictured in your mind, as if it's so. Dreams become real only if you keep them going. Even though you may not see the dream coming true, things are still happening like the animals moving behind the bushes and trees. They're alive. They'll show themselves eventually, unless you stop dreaming. Know this."

"Dreams are energy," Pap-paw would say over and over. "They move. Like water they swiftly seek the path of least resistance. Through the deepest part of your mind (subconscious mind), they hop a ride on the intuitive transportation of your brain. Like the global network of the phone company, the switchboard lights up. They look for connectivity. They seek all of the parts that make it whole. Dreams search for manifestation," he told me.

"What's manifestation?" I asked.

"That's when it becomes real!" he said.

Like an ancient philosopher, my grandfather said, "Dreams travel tirelessly through the subconscious world on the fuel of your relentless intention."

"I don't get it," was my reply.

Narrowing his gaze, he stared into my eyes and said, "If you want and expect it to happen and it's possible, then it will."

Through research and experience, I've learned that dreams can match two people together in a seemingly coincidental manner in order to advance both your purpose and theirs. Dreams collect wants and needs from multiple, unlikely sources and cause unexpected interactions. They can even block dead-end paths, so you'll seek a better route.

A person's dream can delay a walk across the street just enough to meet a person that leads you closer to its fruition. It can sew strangers' thoughts together to weave the finished quilt of your reality. Like a puppeteer pulling the strings behind the scenes, dreams bring your thoughts to life.

"Dreams are alive, just like the woods."

Pap-paw continued his professorial rant and said, "Like a magnet, your dreams attract the needed parts for the finished product. This is what dreams do. They search. They hunt. They repel. They attract. They connect and disconnect. This is all for your benefit Jimmy."

The songwriter's dream of a major hit song scours the universe for the perfect lyric to make it so. A baseball hitter's World Series' dream changes a pitcher's tactics so he can crush the ball during the game's last at bat. My recurrent dream of playing professional tennis and traveling the world created a chance meeting that led to its manifestation. A repeated dream of the qualities of a perfect spouse resulted in one client's wife walking to his front door. And the list goes on from most people I meet. Coincidence? Hardly. Serendipity? Nope. Happenchance? Nada.

I asked many questions of my grandfather. "How long do I dream before I give up?"

He responded with a laugh, "We are stubborn people, Jimmy. We never give up."

"Pap-paw, will I outgrow my dreams? Is it only for kids? Do I try something easier if it doesn't work?"

He laughed from his belly and said, "I still dream, Jimmy, and they absolutely come true."

Yes. Dreams come true! I've witnessed their manifestation thousands of times. They arrive in full regalia with total unpredictability. Some are instant. Some take weeks. Others take decades. A few take a lifetime. Let your subconscious mind work for you behind the scenes. Feed it the pictures of what you want. Stretch the possibilities. There are no rules. Unleash the "24/7 Monster of Make It So." It's especially alive, like the woods at night. Yes...plug in the dream factory before sleep.

Unfortunately, dreams do die. At the first thought of despair, frustration, impatience, exasperation, or aggravation, they flicker and diminish. See it not happening and the dream will instantly start to wither. Slowly, but surely, it will dissipate and be no more.

"I will be one of the world's top #10 tennis players," this young Norwegian hopeful had envisioned since he was a child. Harsh reality exposed that his dream had been covered with extreme doubt, fear, and anxiety with a multitude of excuses. In one visualization exercise, he was to mentally climb over a forty-foot wall that represented all of the challenges blocking his ultimate dream of being dominant in professional tennis. In the middle of this make-believe climb, he opened his eyes, sat up, and blurted out, "I can't do this. I am not good enough. I know I cannot get over the wall." These statements confirmed he was right. He immediately realized his dream had been sabotaged by his own beliefs and expectations.

Dreams kept alive do come true.

When I first met baseball player **Frank Thomas** (a.k.a. Big Hurt) in his first full year (1991) with the Chicago White Sox, I asked him bluntly, "What do you want? Why am I here?" With zero hesitation he boldly stated, "Hall of Fame!"

At this initial meeting, Frank and I talked about opposing pitchers, his hitting approach, the Zone, and his lifelong goals. Finally, Frank lowered his breathing, unhinged his jaw, shut his eyes, and visualized giving his Hall of Fame induction speech in Cooperstown, New York. He literally went to the end of his career in his mind and experienced his soliloquy to the baseball world. Simultaneously, I visualized being in the audience listening to my client's every word.

From our first meeting, Frank Thomas strived to reach his highest standard of performance. "To become a Hall of Famer, you need to be a Hall of Famer every day you play," I demanded. More importantly, Frank demanded this of himself.

The Big Hurt was enormously talented. However, it was his mind-set that lifted him above the other players in the game. This led to him becoming the most fearsome and devastating hitter of his era, while garnering five All-Star selections, four Silver Slugger Awards, two Most Valuable Player awards, and an American League batting title.

Frank Thomas kept his dream alive every day of his career.

More than two decades later, Frank's dream would come true. On July 27, 2014, from the podium at the Hall of Fame induction ceremony, while overlooking the large crowd of friends, family, and fans, Frank said, "A special thanks to my friend and coach, Jim Fannin, I know you're here somewhere, Jim. You told me to live in the Zone, on and off the field and even today, I thank you buddy." As Frank and I both wiped away tears, I thought, "No Frank...thank you! You made your dream come true. I am so proud of you."

As Frank's retirement shifted his focus, this burning desire to be the best of the best still burns brightly. Some things never change. He's

Recipe for a Dream Come True

- Pour in a jug of belief.
- Sprinkle a dash of hope.
- Add a cup of faith.
- Mix in a large spoonful of expectancy.
- Stir hundreds of times with vivid imagination. Remember only "vivid" imagination. No generic.
- Place it finished in your mind at high heat.
- Let it bake overnight.
- Think your dreams alive.

still hitting it out of the park in private business and on the air as a TV baseball analyst.

Keep the dream moving. Keep feeding it. Keep it alive, vibrant, and real in your mind. Believe it will work its invisible magic. Be relentless. See it in finished state. Let your subconscious do its thing. Trust the dream-making process.

If you ever get a chance to walk in the woods, it's a great place to dream. I still do it. Thanks, Pap-paw. I hope your dreams came true.

CHAPTER 2

Think Big—
They Don't Know You

It was my senior year in high school and my senior play was called *The Night of January 16th*. I played elder statesman and wealthy industrialist Bjorn Faulkner. The play focused on a murder trial and there were two separate endings. The audience was the jury and they voted guilty or not guilty, which dictated how we would perform the last act.

With make-up of an older gentleman with graying hair, I proceeded to get in character. Transformed fifty years older than my then current seventeen-year age, I wondered, "What would become of me? Where would I live? What career would I have? What would my wife and children be like? What would I accomplish?" I had many dreams then. I thought big.

What was your biggest dream? Did you accomplish it? If not, does it still rattle around in your mind? Have you given up on it or forgotten it altogether?

What is "thinking big" for you now! What dream is still possible? Does this thought take you out of your comfort zone?

It's not too late! In the last year, I've seen **Casper Wells**, a retired professional baseball player and former Detroit Tiger, return to school to earn his college degree. "Next! I'm ecstatic about the next chapter in my life," Casper exclaims.

Roaming the sidelines of an NFL team was his dream. Unfortunately, talented, passionate, and experienced head football coach **Teddy Keaton** had his career pulled out from under him when his college football program ran out of money and dissolved. He became angry, confused, and had entered negative thinking. "I thought about quitting football altogether," he reluctantly reminisced. He felt his dream had died and could not be resuscitated. His anger led to many negative confrontations and it was this adversity that eventually introduced Teddy to himself. "As an eternal optimist, it's hard to believe I allowed negativity to enter my life," Teddy reflected.

Today, Coach Keaton has rekindled his NFL coaching aspirations and is now a successful, college offense coordinator with NFL coaching potential. "I have recommitted to extreme positivity," he states proudly. "I strive to be in the Zone every day, regardless of the circumstances,

Toyota Park

situations or conditions." As an added bonus, Teddy's renewed spirit attracted the love of his life and marriage is now on the horizon.

Dream big! Make it happen. Even when faced with adversity.

It was a muggy, overcast day in August 2002 and **Steve Landek** (my client and the mayor of Bridgeview, Illinois) was giving me a tour of his 7.5-square-mile fiefdom. Eventually, we drove past open fields of vacant land and I asked, "Who owns this?" and Steve replied, "Bridgeview owns all of this land."

Instantly, a lightning bolt vision of a 20,000-seat outdoor arena popped into my mind. I saw the stadium exterior with fans walking into the venue. I envisioned the field and the packed seats of fanatical fans. "Steve, as the ZoneCoach® to two star players for the Chicago Fire (Major League Soccer franchise), I know they need their own, customized stadium."

"This is the perfect place!"

"Playing in their current home of Soldier Field (where the Chicago Bears play), makes the Fire's 14,000 fans look anemic when seen on television within the iconic 60,000+ seat stadium. Plus, there are no other 20,000-seat arenas in Chicago, and a venue this size could draw world-class concerts, festivals, and other prominent spectator experiences."

Steve laughed out loud bellowing, "You're crazy!"

Maybe I was. "Come on Steve. Shut your eyes, unhinge your jaw, and see your new stadium." With eyes shut and a toothy grin, he replied, "I see it. I see it."

The land where my visual intervention took place is strategically located twelve miles southwest of downtown Chicago. With easy access to major roads, a world-class airport, and one of the greatest cities in the world, this facility could survive and thrive.

Within a few weeks, meetings were orchestrated with my three clients of Bridgeview Bank, Chicago Fire, and the Village of Bridgeview. A deal was struck, money was raised for construction, and a vision was swiftly turning into reality.

On November 30, 2004, the Village of Bridgeview broke ground on the state-of-the-art **Toyota Park** and it officially opened on June 11, 2006. "It is amazing that one thought resulted in a $100 million, 20,000-seat stadium on the south side of Chicago," noted Mayor Landek, "despite the fact that many disbelievers doubted this project from its beginning."

When I attend an event at Toyota Park it is incredible that the former vacant land underneath it was transformed into a venue for the likes of entertainers such as Eric Clapton, B.B. King, Phish, Korn, Kenny Chesney, Pitbull, Jimmy Buffet, Jennifer Lopez, Iggy Azalea, Bob Dylan, Demi Lovato, John Mayer, Slipknot, Chris Brown, Vince Gill, Marilyn Manson, Ariana Grande, and, of course, the Chicago Fire.

Steve Landek is a civic visionary and with his leadership and perseverance this big dream came true.

"You'll never walk again."

The first step is to envision the dream becoming reality. You must see your dream in all its color and hues. Make it real. This step sounds easy. It is not. I know a woman who dreamed big.

Reilley Rankin was a star college golfer. In 1998, she was named the NCAA Freshman of the Year, first-team All-American, Southeastern Conference Champion, and SEC Player of the Year. Then, on June 9, 1999, her life changed.

Acting crazy as college kids can do, Reilley leapt off a sixty-seven-foot cliff (equivalent to the height of a seven-story building) at

Chimney Rock in Lake Martin, Alabama, into the water below. Landing awkwardly, she broke two vertebrae in three pieces and cracked her sternum down the middle. She bruised her heart and lungs and was a half-centimeter from being paralyzed.

Her doctor told Reilley she would never walk again. "You don't know me!" she defiantly thought. Instantly her imagination took over and she remembered visualizing herself as Forrest Gump busting out of his braces. "I will play again," was her prevailing thought.

Visualization is what got Rankin through the toughest 24 months of her life. "As far as I was concerned, I never missed a single day of practice," she said.

Next, you need to commit. This mental step can block or encourage real steps toward your dream. When you move away from your mentally dormant ways, identify the resources needed to advance your vision.

Two years after the accident, and with extreme commitment, Reilley Rankin returned to the University of Georgia and led her team to the 2001 NCAA Championship. But she wasn't done.

Meeting Reilley for the first time, I was in awe of her talent. She was a great athlete. Already an accomplished visualization expert, she saw herself winning her first professional tournament. Day after day we worked on her mental game. Night after night she pictured four prominent letters in her mind.

L.P.G.A.

The pinnacle of women's golf (Ladies Professional Golf Association) was her quest that woke her up in the morning and tucked her into bed at night.

It was May 24, 2003. After walking eighteen holes following my LPGA-hopeful client, Reilley needed a birdie to tie for the lead and secure a play-off spot. When her birdie putt found the bottom of the cup, my heart skipped a beat. On the final play-off hole of the tournament encircled by fans, friends, and me, Reilley won her first professional tournament at the Northwest Indiana Futures Golf Classic, and I cried like a baby as she lifted her coveted prize. This victory turned her nightmare at Lake Martin into a spot on the LPGA Tour.

She rose from a life-threatening injury to the pinnacle of women's golf. Reilley Rankin is one of my heroes.

Most big dreams are stymied because of excuses. Tennis great John McEnroe told me a long time ago, "I've choked many times in my career. Excuses are for losers!" He was right. Tear down your invisible safety net that keeps you from the high wire of possibility. Dreaming big takes a leap of faith. You must believe. You must expect. You must know deep in your heart that you can and will prevail.

Tear down your invisible safety net of excuses.

Take your dreams out of their mental closet. Dust them off and inspect their possibility.

It was in 1974 that I risked every dime in the S.C.O.R.E.® Success System. I was told that I was foolish by the marketing chair at a major university. He looked me in the eye and said, "You will fail. This has never been done." My only thought that afternoon was directed to him, "You don't know me!"

In 1978, I was told that publishing a book was tough. I was warned about the pitfalls and the challenges. Finding a top agent and publishing company were nearly impossible for a first-time author. "You don't know me," I thought. Doubleday published my first book in 1979 and many more would follow. In 1983, I wanted to own an indoor tennis club, but did not have major cash for such a venture. A commercial banker told me, "It is too risky and you don't have enough money." Of course I thought, "You don't know me." I soon owned the 60,000-square-foot S.C.O.R.E.® Indoor Tennis Club and it thrived for sixteen years until it was sold. Dozens of advisors told me, "Coaching out of your sport [tennis] at the highest level is nearly impossible. How could you get started?" Today, I've successfully coached ten professional sports and still do after forty years.

They say NO to big dreams. They? Who are *they*? They are the dream killers. They are the ones that are cowards. They? They are the meek. They are the real ones with no courage. Yes. They are realistic. Yes. They know the odds.

But "they" don't know YOU! Dream big. Good fortune favors the bold.

Dream Board

Swiftly jot down the dreams you've had that you haven't given up on. Allow this list to free-flow from your mind to the paper. Later, you can decide if any or all deserve to be incorporated into The Blueprint.

CHAPTER 3

Go to Higher Ground

L ife can get very confusing and complicated. It is here that dreams can wither and die.

It's easy to get lost within the daily grind of living, working, and playing. Our dreams can get clouded with emotion and placed on the backburner. When you're married, have challenges at work, three young children, and aging, needy parents, life can break the chaos threshold. Simplicity and clarity are both needed to make dreams come true. Here's a look under the mental hood of successful peak performers and dream achievers.

The average person has thousands of thoughts each day with most of them in natural chaos. Our thoughts just ramble from one idea to another. From the time you wake up until you fall asleep, your thought meter climbs with corresponding chaos. On those crazy days when the tail wags the dog, you may have well over 2,000 thoughts. It is these daily thoughts that can either attract or destroy your dreams.

How often do you spend your time worrying about the future or ruminating about the past? In fact, approximately eighty percent of your thoughts vacillate between the past and the future. Only twenty percent of your thoughts are fully engaged in the moment. But the current moment is where peak performance resides.

We're all awake, but not all aware.

This state of full awareness needs to be reversed from twenty percent to eighty percent. Before you were six years old, you were all about "being in the moment." You didn't need to meditate or have a mantra. Your natural blueprint was one of the "here and now." You were locked-in to movement, colors, shapes, and sounds. You noticed everything. You rarely went into the past on your own. In fact, you had little past to consciously archive. You seldom ventured into the future and with no watch, cellphone, or calendar, the future was ONLY for big people, not you. You told the truth as in, "Why are you so fat?" or "Why are your teeth crooked?" If you were tired, you could fall asleep under a clothing rack at the store. If you didn't like your food, you spit it out and screamed, "Yuck!" as loud as you could. You were a free spirit extraordinaire. Your life was in the moment.

Unfortunately, that way of thinking drastically changed when you went to school for the first time. "I told you not to do that" was a statement from an authority figure that jolted you back into the past. The "I told you not to" refrain was bellowed by both teachers and parents. "You'll never amount to anything, if you do that again" is a statement about your future. Quickly, you learn to think about what you don't want. Hmmm...I don't want to be yelled at for no reason. I don't want to be punished. I don't want to feel sad. The list of what you don't want starts to pile up around the age of six.

The quantity of thoughts increases at age six, while the quality of thought declines.

You learn to wield sarcasm to fight people off of your fragile ego. You may have to act like a victim or judge to battle your way to acceptance or to gain a sense of belonging. "I'm an idiot" many learn to say when they screw up. You quickly realize that putting yourself down (first) will typically attract a kind act of, "It's okay. You'll be all right. You're not an idiot." How cool is this self-defense mechanism? It's the first one humans learn in order to cope with failure and regain the care and concern from one of authority. This mechanism is learned by age six and most are still using it at age forty-six.

"If you ever get lost, go to higher ground."

As an adult how do you get above the chaos and think with complete clarity? How do you reduce your thoughts and think like a kid again? Here's what I learned at an early age.

One day Pap-paw told me, "Jimmy, let's play a game of 'find your way home.' It will be exciting. I'm going to put a blindfold over your eyes and take you into the woods to a place you've never been." While this may sound like a scene from a horror movie, my child-self approached the game with excitement and wonder. With this short instruction, he walked me about a mile into the Appalachian hills. He said, "Now count as high as you can and when you believe I'm gone or you get tired of counting, remove the blindfold and figure out how to get back to the house."

The first time we played this game, I was scared and afraid. However, I trusted my grandfather and knew he loved me and would never

allow me to get hurt. If I never returned home, Granny and my parents would make his life miserable. (Of course, he was never far away, as I later learned. He was there just in case.)

"Jimmy, if you ever get lost go to higher ground," he had told me.

"What do you mean, Pap-paw?" I queried.

"It's easy to get turned around in the woods and with everything looking the same, getting lost happens," said Pap-paw. "Even if you mark the trees or lay down breadcrumbs behind you as you walk, getting completely lost is still a possibility."

What do *you* do when lost? Here's what Pap-paw taught me.

First...relax. Know you will find your way home. Look very closely at your surroundings. Adapt swiftly to your circumstance, situation, or condition. Take your time. Breathe deeply. Then seek higher ground so you can see where you've been and see how to get home. Climb a tree. Get up on a big rock. Walk up a hill. From this vantage point above the woods, you can find your way back home. And if there's running water, follow it downstream. You will find other people there and getting home will be easier. "Remember, Jimmy," he would say,

"Go to higher ground when you're lost."

This game of being lost and finding my way home was played out over several years before I was in the third grade. I was taught not to panic. Be cool. Be calm. Figure out how to find a trail or pathway home. Higher ground worked then and it still serves me well, even though I live in a big city.

Similar to being lost in the woods, most of us have been lost in life. This is when you're not sure what to do with your circumstance, situation, or condition. You can be afraid, even fearful. You can think as a victim of your plight. Confusion and indecision can render you immobile. Like an irate judge, getting angry at the people who might have contributed to your predicament can be commonplace. Being lost can paralyze you. However...

Higher ground will help find your way.

This is where your blueprint comes in. In order to find your way to your dreams, a blueprint is mandatory. Venture high above your life. See the different areas where you perform your daily rituals. Looking down from a higher perspective will provide clarity.

As you mentally trace a typical day of your life, it will appear you are simultaneously performing in multiple reality television shows. From work to home and from friends to the gym, life has different venues, actors, set designs, choreography, scripts, and dialogue. As you drive from your home to your work, you can see the family you left behind as you leave the driveway. Soon you're in your company parking lot with a new set of characters awaiting you. One aspect of your life closes as you enter the next. This is your life.

Start creating your blueprint.

On a blank piece of paper, draw no more than eight to ten circles on the page. Make sure the circles do not touch each other. Each circle represents one specific aspect of your life, called an "Arena." Examples are your career, "significant other" relationship, personal finance, self (includes spirituality, health, and wellness), siblings, being a son or daughter to your parents, friends, hobby, and being a mom or dad to your children.

Inside these simple life areas are thoughts about the other people and/or thoughts about your vision and or goals for this aspect of your life. You will also have thoughts about the many area-specific challenges that might arise. All thoughts that pertain to this life segment are housed here. These thoughts are to be managed and contained, if and when a negative situation, condition, or circumstance arises.

For now, identifying your Life Arenas is the goal. As we move through the book, each area will have a well-defined vision with due dates of what you want and corresponding goals and daily routines or tasks. Who are the key people in these arenas and how do they act and interact within this sphere of influence? We will tackle these and other life-specific topics in the upcoming chapters.

Create the blueprint for building your best life possible.

Almost all of my clients came to me for one, specific reason, for one specific area of their life. It typically has been about their business or sport. It is within this primary life section that each had placed most of their "happy eggs." The rest of their life would need to fend for itself. "If I win the Masters, everything will fall into place," confided a PGA golfer. "If I make more money, my challenges at home will be placated and hopefully go away," an investment banker revealed.

Clients flew in from all parts of the world to draft a blueprint for their primary vocation or craft. "Champion" was the quest. Being a champion in EVERY aspect of their life became the realization. This is a true champion.

Even though you probably have a portion of your life that contains most of your thoughts, time, and energy, it is *all of your thoughts in all parts of your life* that are crucial for becoming the master of your destiny.

Managing your thoughts is much easier when your life is segmented into different, stand-alone Life Arenas.

Higher Ground Viewpoint (a few of my clients)

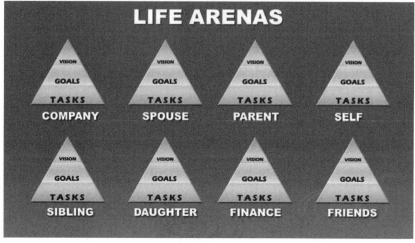

This is a female business owner; married; children; sister; and so on.

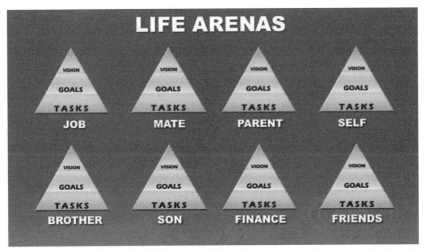

This is a male with a job; girlfriend; children; brothers and sisters; and so forth.

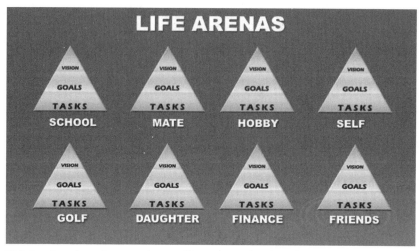

This is a female college student; golfer; current boyfriend; with a hobby (guitar).

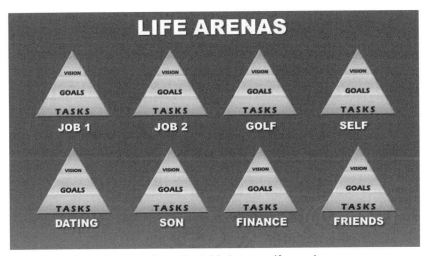

This is a single male; two jobs; only child; dating; golfer; and so on.

My Life Arenas

You will begin to answer, "Who am I?" by segregating your life into independent Life Arenas. Select from a partial, potential list (add, delete, edit as you see fit) of **Self** (everyone has this Arena; includes spirituality, physical wellness, etc.); **Parent; Job** or **Vocation; Second Job; Sibling; Friends; Personal Finance; Golf; Tennis** (other sport); **Son** or **Daughter; Hobby; School; Other Family; Charity;** and **Significant Other** (spouse, mate) Life Arenas. Few Blueprints have more than 10 Life Arenas with most clients opting between 7 to 9 Arenas.

My Life Arenas are:

1.   6.

2.   7.

3.   8.

4.   9.

5.   10.

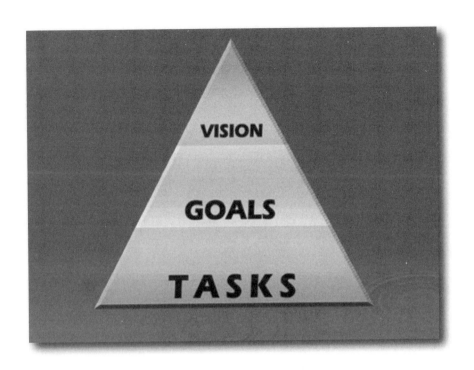

CHAPTER 4

Your Life Arena and Your Thoughts

Christopher Columbus was returning to Spain from the New World in 1492 aboard his single-hull wooden ship, the *Santa Maria*. It was December 24 and Columbus hadn't slept for several days. With a calm sea, he and his steersman decided to sleep while a cabin boy took the helm. With no expert at the wheel, the strong currents carried the ship onto a sandbank, the hull slowly filled with water, and eventually it sank.

Most minds are like the ship, the *Santa Maria*.

Like a single hull ship, we place everything in our mind in one big container. If we have a conflict in our business, the negative residue immediately pours into other parts of our life. As you enter your home, you bellow to anyone that will listen, "Today was a nightmare. I hate my job." From there it's easy to misread the people you love, as everyone scrambles to avoid your gaze. Keep this going and the negative spillage can readily poison the overall home atmosphere. Eventually, one can sink into despair, worry, anxiety, fear, or even depression. This is how a "bad day" happens.

Today's new supertanker ships have divided their hulls into multiple, self-contained compartments. Then, in case a reef or iceberg penetrates this part of the ship, the damage is contained and sealed off so the ship can limp to safe harbor.

Because life is chaotic, each of my clients has segregated his or her life into stand-alone containers called "Life Arenas." A bad experience at work or home can then be contained. Going home happy to see the people you love takes priority and it has nothing to do with business.

The toughest arenas that require the greatest performances are NOT the Masters, Olympics, or the Super Bowl. The arenas that demand the highest standards of human effort are your daily arenas of SELF, FAMILY, FRIENDS, and PROFESSION. You must not take any part of your life for granted, as they all require your focus and attention. These arenas are intangible. They are particular spheres of interest that stand alone, separate, and independent. They contain all of your thoughts, both positive and negative.

Life Arenas collectively contain all your daily thoughts.

Successful Life Arenas have well-defined philosophies, principles, visions, goals, or objectives, with daily tasks and key people. Each Life Arena contains *coaches, co-coaches,* and *players* who perform daily, weekly, or monthly tasks of interaction and action. For example, you can be a coach or leader in your Job Arena and a co-coach with your spouse in your Parent Arena. Also, you could be a player in an entry level Job and a coach in your Sibling Arena because you are the oldest and wisest.

The common denominator for all of these Arena performances is **ATTITUDE**. Your positive or negative mindset dictates your Arena performances.

Beware: There is a tendency to overlap and engulf many Arenas at once. The performance in one Arena can affect the positive or negative performances in another Arena. Non-champions reside here.

Ruth is a great example of this. She's been having challenges at home, in her marriage to Brian. Every morning they have an argument about something minor as they are leaving for work. This spills over to being frustrated with traffic, her fellow drivers, and even the tollbooth collector. By the time she gets to work, Ruth is in a bad mood. Her co-workers see her frown, and begin to avoid her. Her boss gives the better assignments to the employees who are "easier to work with." Her work life suffers, and then, at the end of the day, she deals with the traffic and her marriage challenges again.

Your role in these Life Arenas is either as a *Player, Coach,* or *Co-coach.* Know and understand the *Vision, Goals, Tasks,* and then corresponding **Due Dates** for each Arena. In addition, every Life Arena contains positive or negative Arena influencers called **Key People**.

Prepare to enter each Arena with a fresh "new" attitude. Leave each Arena with an understanding of what transpired, why it transpired, and how you will use the information for self-improvement. Then close the door on this Arena before you enter another.

Ruth needs to clear her mind as she transitions from one Life Arena to another. She needs to take ninety seconds in her car to refocus as she leaves for work. (Some of the exercises in the 90-Second Rule™ can help with this.) This allows Ruth to be more calm on her drive to work, and have a more positive attitude when she gets there. It also allows her to get better assignments and a better work environment. Just because one Arena of her life isn't going well doesn't mean they ALL have to go poorly.

With separate, distinct Life Arenas, you can isolate and contain any negatives and prevent them from spilling over into the rest of your life. Now you are ready to approach your future in an organized manner. By identifying each Arena with the corresponding *Vision, Goals, Tasks* (and due dates), and *Key People*, you will no longer take a segment of your life for granted.

For the peak performer, only one Life Arena typically is his or her **Primary Arena**. This is the Arena where you spend the vast majority of your time, energy, and sometimes money. This is not to say it's the most important Arena; it's just the one that occupies the majority of your thoughts.

The Vision for the Primary Arena usually wakes up the champion and puts him or her to bed at night. Of course, your Primary Arena can swiftly change. If your child is ill or you're playing your golf club championship this weekend, then perhaps this Arena will temporarily become your Primary Arena. Primary Arenas can change depending on your life circumstances, conditions, and situations.

Once your life is organized into Arenas, it becomes a *Vision Board* for targeted imagery or visualization. It also becomes a *Thought Manager* for staying aware of real and potential challenges, before they fester and turn into negatives.

It's your life. Organize it and GO FOR IT!

CHAPTER 5

Do You Have
Well-Defined Life Visions?

My first book, *Tennis & Kids: The Family Connection*, first appeared in my mind as a vision. I mentally pictured moms and dads with their children, utilizing drills and exercises from the book. With these images in mind of parents focused on leveraging their children's talents, I was inspired to manifest this scenario into reality. This vision woke me up and placed me in bed at night. I had a well-defined vision. This spawned a hardcover book that found its place in libraries throughout the country and turned my vision into reality.

You are more than your job or career.

Paul Rakovic was training to become a master sommelier in Las Vegas. The world of wine was competitive and the knowledge and experience required to become a wine expert was daunting. His career path was organized, but a coincidental encounter introduced him to the digital marketing world, and suddenly that resonated with him. The thought of owning a digital marketing company grew stronger and stronger. It began occupying mental storage that had been only reserved for cabernets, merlots, and zinfandels.

"Do I give up my career path of becoming a master sommelier?" Paul pondered. "The world of the sommelier is labor intensive and not as lucrative as I had thought. The hours are long and the business demands my nights and this cuts into my parenting time with two little ones," he confided to me.

Finally with a leap of faith this "master sommelier to be" moved from Las Vegas to Colorado and shelved his skill for decanting great wines to marketing content on the Internet. He had crafted a well-defined vision. After a thorough examination on this different, but highly competitive industry, Paul stated with confidence, "If the people I researched can do it, I know I can do it."

Even though Paul's multimillion dollar, digital marketing business is a thriving reality, he knows he's more than a digital marketer.

Mel Gibson is a great actor and director with many memorable performances under his belt that made him a household name. After a long dinner in a private California restaurant setting, Mel conveyed his love for movies and especially moviemaking to me. "I love movies," he gleefully stated. "I love all of the creativity needed from so many people and tying their expertise together in a seamless quilt of cinema excites me," he said. "Plus, there is nothing more enjoyable than taking a book or script and make it come alive, regardless if it happened 100 years ago or, 100 years from now. Imagination and creativity are intoxicating."

Listening to Mel speak about directing revealed his childlike passion for creating an audience experience that lasts long after people leave the theater. Being the ultimate bandleader of make-believe had become his ultimate vision. Turning this vision into reality is now his obsessive quest. With *The Passion of the Christ*, *Apocalypto*, and *Hacksaw Ridge* under his belt, he is on his way to a legendary movie director's career. Most of all, Mel knows he's much more than a director.

Each successful life arena requires a well-defined Vision.

Each arena vision is a dream or daydream that has stepping-stone goals with corresponding daily tasks, all to be completed within a stringent timeline. Every dream that turned into reality had this process, whether it was created consciously or subconsciously.

Dozens of world champions were interviewed in the late 1970s and a common thread was found. Each champion had a graphic image of his or her vision that motivated, inspired, and stimulated him or her. None of the champions had visions for each part of their life.

When things didn't go their way, the champion uses their inspirational vision to carry their tired bodies and take control of their overtaxed minds. When adversity arrives, it is the champion's vision that answers the door. The vision replaces and blankets all negative thoughts. This mental image becomes the symbol of the champion's success. But what about the other aspects of life?

A positive vision is all about what you want and need in your life. This mental image dictates your thoughts and actions. It gives you joy and keeps you away from pain and displeasure. Unfortunately, like a weed that can overrun a garden, your Primary Vision cannot control all of your thoughts in life. This is like placing all your "happy eggs" in one basket, which we know is an unwise investment. Every client has been told, "You're more than a professional athlete" or "You're more than a businessperson."

Most successful achievers have a Primary Vision. As discussed, this dominant image takes up the majority of time, energy and (even) money. This doesn't mean it's the most important Life Arena. It's just the Arena that is the most significant at this time. A business owner has a Primary Vision of $10,000,000 in gross sales. All of his or her thoughts cascade into this hopeful and expectant reality. Even though it consumes the majority of time and effort, it is still not as important as his or her Spouse, Parent, or Self Arenas.

Your Primary Arena can and will change during your life. Sometimes it can change swiftly. If your wife becomes gravely ill, the Spouse Arena instantly becomes your Primary Arena. If your oldest child is struggling with grades and has been caught with illegal drugs, this becomes your Primary Arena.

Each of your Life Arenas needs a Vision that dictates the action and interaction within this sphere of interest. A dominant Primary Arena can cause neglect in the rest of your life. Like an abandoned home, the house can begin to decay. It eventually will showcase the wear and tear. With Life Arenas, this decay reveals itself with bickering, anger, apathy, rudeness, disrespect, impoliteness, vulgarity, stubbornness, sarcasm, hostility, and other negative traits.

Once per week, peruse your life from Higher Ground and picture the multiple Visions in your life. Continue to focus on your Primary Arena. Just refuse to neglect the other aspects of your life.

Sample Life Arena Visions

Following is an example of Life Arena Visions. In later chapters, we will address your specific Arenas in more depth. A few examples of a Vision for each Arena are:

- **Self Arena**—Vision: Physically Fit
  Due Date: _____

- **Parent Arena**—Vision: World-Class, Decision-Maker Son
  Due Date: _____

- **Personal Finance Arena**—Vision: $1,000,000 Net Worth
  Due Date: _____

- **Spouse/Mate Arena**—Vision: Best Husband Possible
  Due Date: _____

- **Friends Arena**—Vision: Best Companion Possible
  Due Date: _____

- **Sibling Arena**—Vision: #1 Supporter
  Due Date: _____

- **Son/Daughter Arena**—Vision: Best Son Possible
  Due Date: _____

- **Career/Job Arena**—Vision: Company President
  Due Date: _____

Choose Your Life Visions

Arena	Vision	Due Date
1. Self		
2.		
3.		
4.		
5.		
6.		
7.		
8.		
9.		
10.		

CHAPTER 6

Meet Mr. Wish, Mr. Want, and Mr. Need

In order to ensure your Visions become reality, please meet three fictional car salesmen. They work for the same dealership. Their names are **Wish**, **Want**, and **Need**. All three have the same experience and knowledge about cars. Each has the same monthly quota and the same experience on the job. All produced different results this month.

Wish would like to sell a lot of cars. He rarely does. He has plenty of excuses and blame for why he can't close a sale. He missed the quota. **Want** narrows his focus at the end of the month to barely make his quota. But he makes it. Lastly, **Need** chips away every day at his goal. He exceeds the quota while breaking the dealership record.

What are the differences in their thinking?

Wish wishes he could reach the quota. His wishes contain no substance of sales processes and work ethic. The quota, inadvertently, becomes his ceiling. He places a psychological safety net underneath himself in case he falls. The net, which will catch his ego, is built with excuses and blame. He wears the nametag of the victim and the judge. He ridicules the sales manager. He puts down customers behind their backs. He wields sarcasm like a knife on his peers. He mocks **Want**. He despises **Need**. Every prospective customer can feel his negativity and last-minute desperation. They resist even his best pitches. He'll soon be on the streets looking for another job. "I used to work there. Their systems are terrible. Management doesn't get it," he'll probably say about the place, to anyone that will listen.

Want believes he'll make the quota. However, his push at the end of the month repels a few savvy buyers. He still prevails. He is a journeyman. He gets by now with the minimum effort. However, he looks and acts the part when needed. He has been bypassed multiple times for the sales manager position. He holds resentment and grudges. His best years are in the rear-view mirror. He tells stories of the good ol' days and brings up how they used to do it. He has settled. He despises **Need**. "Who does he think he is?" laments **Want**.

Need expects to be the leader. He expects to blow by the quota at mid-month. Management sets quotas for the average and below average personnel. **Need** knows this. His mind is on setting records. He sees the goal clearly. He has mapped out his month with precise strategies and tactics. He chips away every day at the record with unbridled confidence. This need to be the record-holder gets him up in the morning and puts him to bed at night. "One day I'll have my own dealership," he thinks to himself. The buyers love his confidence. They buy from **Need**.

Wish, **Want**, and **Need** handle stress differently. Let's look under the mental hood of our three car salesmen.

We react to stress in two ways. Stress, which produces cortisol in our bodies, is the ignition fuel for peak performance. We can create it on our own terms and conditions. It can motivate us and lift us up. By setting our own goals and timelines, stress can drive us to greatness. Or stress can bring us to our knees with crippling force. We can choke on it. It can depress the confident, slow down the grizzled veteran and disable the special talent. Even champions have fallen victim to the cruelty of stress. It can ravage our bodies. With muscles tight from stress it can trigger sickness and disease. Stress can kill. Without it, however, our achievements will be mediocre at best.

Wish has a chip on his shoulder. His judge and victim demeanor mask his insecurity and lack of confidence. His beef is focused outward without looking inward. He wishes he were making more money but his effort is inconsistent. He seldom trains. He tells his wife only what is wrong at the dealership. He does it so much, she is finally glad he no longer works there. She has, unwittingly, become an enabler. This cycle will continue until she catches on and busts him out or until he morphs into **Need**.

"I wish to sell cars!" Wishes lack structure. Seldom is there a plan of strategy and tactics with a wish. Wishes typically wait for something to happen. Wishes attract more wishes. "I wish to buy a car."

Want has procrastinated all his life. He believes he can pull it off no matter what. However, the last minute rush is mentally draining. The first 10 days of the next month are spent replenishing his energy. There is little sense of urgency until quota time rolls around again. This roller-coaster cycle is very difficult to change. He doesn't know how to get off this endless track.

"I want to sell cars!" A want usually lacks power from within. Commitment is seldom there. Most "Wants" skip the process needed for achievement. Wants attract more wants. "I want to buy a car."

Need sells himself on himself. He makes positive deposits in his optimistic bank account every day while **Wish** and **Want** make withdrawals. **Need** has a need to be the best at every phase of the sales process. This translates in studying the competition. He knows his product line inside and out. He knows his customer base. He needs to improve your quality of transportation at a price you can afford. This attracts your need to buy a car. **Need** knows you. He knows himself. He needs to know.

"I need to sell cars!" This need permeates all of the process. It comes from deep inside. There is conviction when a need is present. A need has purpose. A need demands. A need is essential. **Needs** attract more needs. "I need to buy a car."

A wish and a want ricochet within your mind.
A need finds a permanent place in your heart.

Now you know the difference between a wish, a want, and a need.

The following chapter, **Focus on the Big Rocks**, is about finding macro goals that are **NEEDED** to make dreams come true.

CHAPTER 7

Focus on the Big Rocks!

To understand the macro and micro aspects of life, business, and sports, the concept of Big Rocks will make the point. Big Rocks are **NEEDED** to turn Visions into reality. This is all about goal-setting. All **Visions** need stepping-stone-like **Goals** that lead to the manifestation of a positive reality.

Mentally or physically place a one-gallon, wide-mouthed, glass jar in front of you. The jar represents your overall Life. Carefully place about a dozen fist-sized rocks, one at a time, into the jar. These Big Rocks represent the major components in your life. Your significant other is a Big Rock. Your vision for your company is a Big Rock and so is each of your children. Make sure a Big Rock representing your wellness is in there. When the jar is filled to the top and no more rocks can fit inside, ask yourself...

"Is the jar full?"

The jar is NOT full. Next, dump some gravel into the jar and shake the jar, causing pieces of gravel to work themselves down into the spaces between the Big Rocks. These smaller rocks are important in your life, but not as important as the Big Rocks. If being the president of your company is a Big Rock, then the gravel might be reaching and or exceeding your sales quota.

"Is the jar full?"

The jar is NOT full. Now take out a bucket of sand. This represents even more life minutia. Dump the sand in the jar. The grains of sand filter into all of the spaces left between the rocks and the gravel.

Once more ask yourself, "Is the jar full?"

The jar is NOT full. Finally, grab a pitcher of water and began to pour until the jar is filled to the brim. The drops of water represent even less significant items in your life. This could include getting a haircut or talking to a supplier about an order mix-up.

"Is the jar full?" Without splitting the atom, let's say it's full.

"What is the point of this illustration?"

Possible answers are "No matter how full your schedule seems, if you try really hard you can always fit some more in it!" and another is "You can pack a lot of crap into your life" or "You can fill your day with things that do not translate to the bottom line and the success of the company."

However, that's not the point. The truth this illustration teaches is:

If you don't put the Big Rocks in first, there will be no room for the Big Rocks.

Champions in life, business, and sports think daily about their Big Rocks. What are the Big Rocks in your life? What are the Big Rocks at work? What are the Big Rocks in your sport? These are the Big Rocks for most people. It is your children, loved ones, education, worthy cause, teaching or mentoring others, doing things you love, time for yourself, your health, your significant other, financial freedom, Masters green jacket, and the like.

In business, the Big Rocks are working on the projects that matter. These are the ones that impact the bottom line, growth, and so on. It's the macro issues that drive the business to prosperity. It's your pipeline, your hiring, your training, your Vision, your closing ratio, and your client track record.

In life, the Big Rocks are your wellness, financial security, personal income stream, children, best friends, mother and father, and so forth.

In sports, the Big Rocks are fairways in regulation, your putting stroke, the club championship, peaking at The Masters, your field goal shooting percentage, batting average, or your first serve percentage.

A Big Rock for the year is not necessarily a Big Rock for the month, week, or day. Big Rocks are simply macro goals that are well defined, realistic, achievable, and measurable.

Remember to put these BIG ROCKS in first or you'll never get them in at all. Stay away from the gravel, sand, or water. If you flood your mind with the little stuff (the gravel, the sand, the water), then your life will be filled with little things you worry about that don't really matter. You'll never have the real quality time needed to spend on the big, important stuff (Big Rocks).

Choose your Big Rocks wisely.

After you've selected a singular Vision for each of your Life Arenas, then create Arena Big Rock stepping-stones. What are the Big Rocks in your Life Visions? What are the Big Rocks in your career? What are the

Big Rocks for your sport? Put those in your jar first. Big Rocks will lead you to your Vision, and your dream now will come true.

Big Rocks are macro goals that are crucial for your success. They will inspire, motivate, stimulate, and encourage your daily action. Set them carefully and wisely. Make them concise and clear. They need to be achievable within your timeline. Choose no more than five Big Rocks per Vision. Fewer will be easier to accomplish and will produce better results.

With each Life Arena, there are Visions that you want to fulfill. It's the Big Rocks accomplished over time that lead to these Visions and this can place you on a stepping-stone pathway to greatness.

Life Arena Big Rock Examples

Self Arena
Vision: Physically Fit
Possible Big Rocks: Weigh 185 lbs.; 10 percent body fat; 100 oz. H_2O daily; 2,000 calories; eliminate sugar.

Parent Arena
Vision: World-Class, Decision-maker Son
Possible Big Rocks: He prepares (on his own) for school; he decides which sport to play; he provides dinner choices.

Personal Finance Arena
Vision: $1,000,000 Net Worth
Possible Big Rocks: Save $500/monthly; invest in 401(k); purchase rental property; refinance home.

Spouse/Mate Arena
Vision: Best Husband Possible
Possible Big Rocks: Adhere to the 90-Second Rule™ when coming home; Take 90 seconds to relax and breathe when I don't get my way; always make date night; avoid talking over her with company present.

Friends Arena
Vision: Empathetic, compassionate companion
Possible Big Rocks: Acknowledge milestones; guys' night out; ask better questions.

Sibling Arena:
Vision: #1 Supporter
Possible Big Rocks: Attend all sporting events; know their dreams and goals; always lend a helping hand; communicate weekly.

Son/Daughter Arena

Vision: Best Son Possible

Possible Big Rocks: Plan anniversary surprise; help parents refinance home; ask questions about their individual and collective future; memorialize an interview about their past.

Career/Job Arena

Vision: Company President

Possible Big Rocks: Think macro; take leadership course; hire executive coach; delegate; implement Big Rock report.

What Are Your Big Rocks?

Fill in your Arenas, Vision, and create the Big Rocks needed to manifest your Vision into reality. Keep it short and simple. Less is more.

1. Self

2.

3.

4.

5.

6.

7.

8.

9.

10.

CHAPTER 8

Champions Are Fastidious. Are You?

Now you know that the best in the world have a Vision that wakes them up in the morning and tucks them in at night. They have Big Rocks to be accomplished every quarter, month, week, and day. However, these high achievers are also fastidious in the daily tasks that crush the Big Rocks that lead to their Vision.

What does that mean? It means that high achievers are very attentive to accuracy and detail. There's a big difference between doing something and doing it well. It's not enough to be "good." Being focused on accuracy and detail will help make you "great."

Champion performers are experts at some aspect of their sport or field. NBA superstar **Stephen Curry** of the world champion Golden State Warriors is an expert at shooting a basketball. This expertise was honed by launching 500 shots every day in the off-season. During the NBA's grueling season, he daily fires up 250 to 300 balls. More importantly, it's his approach (not the quantity of shots) that sets him apart. He is fastidious.

Fastidious: very attentive and concerned about accuracy and detail.

Years ago I had a meeting with the Chicago Blackhawks General Manager in the old Chicago stadium. As I entered the sports arena around noon, I heard a lone basketball bouncing on the hardwood. Later that night the Chicago Bulls would play the Boston Celtics and there on the floor alone was Celtic great **Larry Bird.** He dribbled two steps to his right and swiftly launched a three-point shot. Over and over, Bird shot the *same* shot with the *same* precision and attention to detail. After a forty-five-minute meeting with the Chicago Black-hawks' late, great player and then GM **Keith Magnuson,** I found Bird still shooting the same shot. Later that night, I witnessed Larry Legend drain this same shot with only seconds left in the game to force the Bulls into overtime. He was fastidious.

To prepare for his first appearance on *The Tonight Show*, comedian **Jerry Seinfeld** did two hundred reps of his routine. This master of detail in crafting a joke is fastidious!

Here's another example. The **Longo Toyota** dealership in El Monte, California, has been one of the best Toyota dealers in the country for years. They are well known for their attention to detail. If you ever visit, check out their legendary line-up of new and used cars. Each is spaced from the other with exact precision. They are fastidious.

In the late '70s, I coached the third-best tennis player in the world. We spent hours and hours working on one shot...a topspin backhand lob. This seldom used shot would definitely come in handy as **Adriano Panatta's** backhand was being attacked by most of the Tour players. "I need this shot," stated Panatta. For sixty-days, the new shot was kept under wraps, as it was only executed in drills and practice matches. Finally, against the world's #1 player at the time, **Jimmy Connors,** Panatta struck the perfect topspin backhand lob in the final set to defeat the world's most formidable foe. After this shot was executed and the ball bounced inside the baseline and away from the back-pedaling Connors, Adriano turned to me in the stands, smiled, nodded, and fist pumped with satisfaction. Being fastidious was the difference.

Peter Haleas is the chairman of Bridgeview Bank in Chicago. He inherited a fledgling and modest suburban bank with no more than $150 million in assets, which was about the size of a branch of Chase Bank. However, Peter had a Vision of a $1.5 billion bank in five years and he knew he could not do it alone. With bank president **Bill Conaghan,** they embarked on an internal marketing and public relations campaign for their small banking team.

Two routines occurred regularly. First, every employee meeting regardless of the number of participants was started with, "We are a $1.5 billion bank." Soon, the bank employees began to act like it. Peter and Bill became fastidious in this detail of framing all meetings. Second, they created Bridgeview's mission statement and both committed it to memory. With cash denominations of tens, twenties, fifties, and hundreds, both patrolled the bank with each seeking employees who knew the mission statement verbatim. "For $20, who knows the bank mission statement?" queried Bill as he scoured a meeting. "For $100, who knows our mission statement?" asked Peter as he sought takers of a crisp Benjamin. These random acts of unity and bonding solidified the bank mindset, and five years later the vision of $1.5 billion in assets (with record return on assets) was reached. **Peter Haleas** and **Bill Conaghan** were fastidious.

There is a cost to being great.
It's paying attention to detail.

What is your strength in parenting, relationships, management, sales, golf, or other sport? What aspect of your business, sport, or life do you need to hone?

Champions definitely have dominant aspects of their game. It is these strengths that are refined with precision, tenacity and perseverance. However, it is the approach of committing to excellence that is the difference maker.

After a meeting in Chicago's **Waldorf Astoria Hotel,** I walked down the hallway and noticed a discarded piece of paper on the floor. A manager silently swept in like an eagle after a fish and with a nod and a smile placed the wastepaper into his pocket. How many employees would have dismissed the paper on the floor and walked by it? Not at one of the world's great hotels! Cleanliness mattered to him. It was not his official job. This manager had pride in his work and he paid attention to detail.

NFL All-Pro quarterback and former client **Scott Mitchell** played as a rookie for the great Miami Dolphins coach **Don Shula.** After one Wednesday practice, Scott asked the Coach, "Are we still doing the same thing this Wednesday?"

Shula replied, "On Wednesday in the 1970s, 1980s, and the 1990s, practice has had the same schedule and routines. Any more questions?" As the coach of the only undefeated, world champion NFL team, Shula was fastidious.

New York Yankee star and long-time client **Alex Rodriguez** retired in 2016 at the age of forty-two. A-Rod has repeated the same affirmation thousands of times before and during every game. "I hit solid!" he repeated to himself with confidence. His consistent, thorough, and fastidious mental approach to hitting produced excellence throughout his entire career.

Well-executed mental and physical routines produce great parents, lasting relationships, master chefs, Hall of Fame athletes, world-class musicians, great actors, and successful entrepreneurs. What about you?

Champions in sports, business, and life tirelessly hone the basics of their craft.

What fundamental or basic in your business or sport can you hone into an expertise? Have you drained 100, four-foot putts in a row in pursuit of a dominant short game? The best putters in the world do this regularly. Do you relentlessly practice the opening and closing of your sales presentation? The greatest sales personnel do. Do you greet your "significant other" with full engagement and your most positive demeanor every time after you've been apart for a few hours or more? The best spouses never waver.

The world is tired of mediocrity. Experts are wanted and needed. It's time to practice the basics of your craft. Your approach of committed excellence will be the difference in becoming and staying a champion.

Several years ago I presented a seminar to twenty-two district managers of **Dominick's Finer Foods**, a former Chicago-based grocery chain. The least-tenured manager had seventeen years under his belt. It was obvious they were not interested in honing their craft of managing excellence within their team. Why should they? They were veterans. What more could they learn? They knew it all. They have been there and done that. However, I intuitively knew their days were numbered. Within six months, Dominick's was purchased by national grocery chain Safeway and all managers were released. They were NOT fastidious.

Experts keep training. They strive for excellence. They hone the basics and are obsessed with accuracy, consistency, and quality. They pay attention to detail. They are fastidious in executing their daily tasks that lead to the Big Rocks that will take them to their Vision.

Are you fastidious?

This is NOT your typical to-do list. This Task Sheet will NEVER have *get a haircut, pick up milk,* or *go to the cleaners.* Tasks relate to the basics of your Life Arenas. These tasks or units of work will help you accomplish the Big Rocks that will lead you to your Vision.

Self Arena
Vision: Physically fit
Possible Big Rocks: Weigh 185 lbs.; twenty percent body fat; 100 oz. H_2O daily.
Possible Tasks: Visualize tomorrow's food intake the night before; purchase H_2O container; walk three miles daily (7:00 a.m.); purchase new walking shoes; consume 1,750 calories daily.

Parent Arena
Vision: World-class, Decision-maker Son
Possible Big Rocks: Choose his own clothes for school; let him decide which sport to play; he provides dinner choices.
Possible Tasks: Take son shopping; try out for soccer; teach risk and reward principles.

Personal Finance Arena
Vision: $1,000,000 Net Worth
Possible Big Rocks: Save $500/monthly; invest in 401(k); purchase rental property; refinance home.
Possible Tasks: Interview three CPAs; dismiss financial planner; see four properties with realtor.

Spouse/Mate Arena
Vision: Best Husband Possible
Possible Big Rocks: Adhere to the 90-Second Rule™ (90SR) when coming home; take ninety seconds to relax and breathe when I don't get my way; always make date night; avoid talking over her with company present.
Possible Tasks: Place 90SR sticker on dashboard; book next Friday's dinner and play; practice breathing six to eight breaths per minute.

Friends Arena
Vision: Best Friend Possible
Possible Big Rocks: Acknowledge milestones; guys' night out.
Possible Tasks: Join tennis league; book fishing charter; make Christmas list.

Sibling Arena
Vision: Best Brother Possible
Possible Big Rocks: Attend all sporting events; know their dreams and goals; always lend a helping hand.
Possible Tasks: Share Golf in the Zone™ CD; go to Ohio State vs. Michigan football game; avoid yelling at siblings.

Son/Daughter Arena
Vision: Best Son Possible
Possible Big Rocks: Plan anniversary surprise; memorialize an interview about their past.
Possible Tasks: Conference call re: surprise party; purchase anniversary gift.

Career/Job Arena

Vision: Company President

Possible Big Rocks: Think macro; take leadership course; hire executive coach; lead by example.

Possible Tasks: Teach Big Rocks concept; book leadership course for the first Tuesday next month; research and interview three executive coaches by end of month.

CHAPTER 9

Who Is Influencing Your Life?

Momma was right. Birds of a feather flock together. And...you are the friends you keep. You are the mirror image of your friends. She warned us:

Turning The Blueprint into reality will involve other people.

My then-teenaged daughter had her newfound boyfriend arrive unannounced to the house. I remember this clearly. He and I had never met. Wow! He had a size 20-inch neck, or so it seemed. And he looked like he could bash a few beer cans on his forehead. Was I pre-judging? Of course, I was. He's coming to visit my baby. In fact, he did have over a dozen concussions from football. He was unruly, rude, and utterly... well you get the point. Unfortunately, my teenaged beauty didn't listen. She eventually allowed this boyfriend to affect her grades and her competitive tennis in a very negative way.

In short...people influence other people. Influence is a win-win proposition. It's manipulation that is win-lose, and many people are manipulating when they believe they are influencing.

Who are the Key People in your life?

Who are these people that can and do impact our decisions and our life? Most of us have anywhere from ten to fifty Key People who directly and or indirectly influence or manipulate how we think, dress, act, speak, and even manage our money.

Key People are either influential or manipulative people in your life. They can positively and or negatively influence your thoughts and you can do the same to them. Key People could be family members, friends, co-workers, or associates. They could be your doctor, life coach, clergyman, physical trainer, attorney, or accountant. Key People can and do affect your different Life Arenas.

Key People are coaches or guides, players or participants, and even co-coaches within your Life Arenas. Some will be proactive while others may be passive. Many will be positive as they seek solutions to challenges and others will think and act in a doom and gloom manner, regardless of the situation, circumstance, or condition.

After understanding the Key People in your life, you may need to:
- ► Co-exist peacefully
- ► Distance from them totally
- ► Change them in a positive way

A few of these individuals will be a part of your private *Inner Circle*. This very select group has definite influence on your goal attainment. Typically, this small group of people is limited to five people or fewer. Manipulators must be kept from this private inner sanctum. Most successful companies have a Board of Directors that review financial statements, network, and advise them on the future of the entity they serve. Your Inner Circle needs to operate the same way.

Whose advice do you seek before you make a major life move? Do you draw from different viewpoints before you make the final decision? Select this group for their non-emotional objectivity regarding your macro goals. Trust them to be confidential.

What do Key People influence or manipulate? It's your thoughts and actions, and the thoughts and actions of other people in the Arena. You can be impacted by what they say or don't say.

How many times have you had an idea and run it by different people in your life? "I'm thinking of going back to school." The thoughts and actions of other people in your life can influence your own actions. One person might say, "Go back to school?! Why would you want to do that? You're too old to go back to school. You want to sit there in a classroom with a bunch of kids, and do homework again?" Another person might say, "That's a great idea! I can just see you in the classroom getting energy and ideas from the other students. Let's look for some different programs for you to consider." Clearly, the second person is one you want to have in your Inner Circle, and the first person is one that needs to be further out.

Specifically, Key People can impact the individual components of your attitude. Your individual levels of **Self-discipline**, **Concentration**, **Optimism**, **Relaxation**, and **Enjoyment** (**S.C.O.R.E.**®) can rise or fall depending on how you interact and react to your Key People. Example: Your boss in your Job Arena can increase your Optimism by paying you a compliment for a job well done. The next day this same person can affect your Relaxation and Enjoyment level by giving you a difficult task with an unreasonable deadline. Consequently, a Key Person can impact your overall attitude and ultimately your performance.

If you allow a person in your Job Arena to negatively affect your thoughts, he or she can become an attitude breaker or S.C.O.R.E.° Breaker. If a person motivates or inspires you at work, he or she is an attitude maker or S.C.O.R.E.° Maker. A Key Person can influence you in a positive way and or manipulate you in a negative manner, all within a matter of seconds.

Attitude Maker: This person has a positive impact on you. They add value to the Arena. This person reflects positivity with words, deeds, and/or body language.

Attitude Breaker: This person has a negative impact on you. They subtract value from the Arena. This person reflects negativity with words, deeds, and/or body language. Some attitude breakers or S.C.O.R.E.° Breakers are unaware of their negative impact. They may have a hidden agenda of which they are not fully aware. Beware of this person. Filter what they say.

In the previous example where you talked about going back to school, the first person is an Attitude Breaker. They may think they are being "helpful" by allowing you to see the "reality" of the situation. But really, all they are doing is negatively affecting your attitude. The second person is an Attitude Maker. They aren't concerned with THEIR opinion of your goals. They are concerned with helping YOU achieve what you want.

Sometimes an individual can be a Key Person in more than one Life Arena. In fact, a Key Person can simultaneously be a **Maker** or **Breaker** in multiple Arenas. Example: Your "significant other" is obviously a Key Person in your **Significant Other** Arena, but they are also influential in your **Parent** Arena, or your **Self** Arena where they are assisting you in losing weight.

Each of your Life Arenas contains your thoughts and the other Key People's thoughts. This can make some Arenas complex and difficult to manage. If an Arena is overly negative, understand whose thoughts need to change in order to turn it into a positive.

Know the Key People in your life.

Make a list of your Key People. Ascertain the Makers and Breakers within each Arena. From the Maker group, select your private Inner Circle. Keep your Inner Circle an odd number of people in case you want them to vote for a specific solution. Meet with them collectively once every quarter or at least once a year.

Who is influencing your life? You are. The possible Key People in your life will soon be showcased. You will also be armed with concrete tools, techniques, and tips to be a positive influencer. Be a **Maker** for all of your Key People and leverage their strengths to impact your Big Rocks and Visions.

As you build your customized Life Blueprint know that YOU influence YOU. However, there are approximately ten to fifty Key People who will help or hinder your success. You must be your own best friend as you create this master document. It will act as your guide to a successful life and your genuine, authentic best self.

Self Arena
Vision: Physically fit
Big Rocks: Weigh 185 lbs.; 20% body fat; 100 oz. H_2O daily.
Tasks: Visualize food intake the night before; purchase H_2O container; walk three miles daily; purchase new walking shoes; consume 1,750 calories daily.
Possible Key People: Spouse; significant other; physical trainer; minister; priest; doctor; pharmacist; nutritionist; parent; counselor; friends; psychologist; psychiatrist.

Parent Arena
Vision: World-Class, Decision-maker Son
Big Rocks: Choose clothes for school; make sports decisions; provide dinner choices; self-discipline at school; great morning attitude.
Tasks: Take son shopping; try out for soccer; teach risk and reward.
Possible Key People: Siblings; teachers; coaches; spiritual advisors; counselor; psychologist; psychiatrist; other parent; grandparents; other relative.

Personal Finance Arena
Vision: $1,000,000 net worth
Big Rocks: Save $500/monthly; invest in 401(k); purchase rental property; refinance home; draft will; create budget; create will.
Tasks: Interview three CPAs; dismiss financial planner; see four properties with Realtor; place finances on QuickBooks.
Possible Key People: Financial advisor; insurance agent; stockbroker; HR advisor; CPA; attorney; banker; parent; real estate agent.

Spouse/Mate Arena
Vision: Best Husband Possible
Big Rocks: Adhere to the 90-Second Rule™ (90SR) when coming home; take ninety-seconds to relax and breathe when I don't get my way; always make date night; avoid talking over her with company present.
Tasks: Place 90SR sticker on dashboard; book next Friday's dinner and play; practice breathing six to eight breaths per minute.
Possible Key People: Spiritual advisor; priest; parent; best friend; significant other; spouse; counselor; psychologist.

Son/Daughter Arena

Vision: Best Son Possible
Big Rocks: Plan anniversary surprise; ask questions about their individual and collective future; memorialize and interview their past; research senior living; manage medical care; bolster confidence.
Tasks: Sibling conference call to finalize surprise party; purchase parents' anniversary gift; talk with doctor; fix parents' gutters; mow their lawn.
Possible Key People: Siblings; parents' friends; doctor; grandparents.

Career/Job Arena

Vision: Company President
Big Rocks: Think macro; take leadership course; hire executive coach; delegate; implement Big Rock Report.
Tasks: Teach Big Rocks; book leadership course for the first Tuesday next month; research and interview three executive coaches by end of month.
Possible Key People: Boss; co-workers; HR staff; spouse; direct reports; board of directors; executive coach.

Friends Arena

Vision: Best Friend Possible
Big Rocks: Celebrate milestones; guys' night out; fishing trip; join tennis league; send Christmas gifts.
Tasks: Join indoor tennis club; book fishing charter; make Christmas list.
Possible Key People: Other friends; spouse or significant other.

Sibling Arena

Vision: Best Brother Possible

Big Rocks: Attend all sporting events; know their dreams and goals; always lend a helping hand.

Tasks: Share Golf in the Zone™ CD; go to football game together (Friday); avoid yelling next meeting.

Possible Key People: Other siblings; parents; grandparents; aunts; uncles; sibling's friends; sibling's spouse; sibling's children.

Your Life Blueprint

Arena: Self

Vision:

Due Date:

Big Rocks:

Tasks:

Key People:

Arena:

Vision:

Due Date:

Big Rocks:

Tasks:

Key People:

Arena:

Vision:

Due Date:

Big Rocks:

Tasks:

Key People:

Arena:

Vision:

Due Date:

Big Rocks:

Tasks:

Key People:

Arena:

Vision:

Due Date:

Big Rocks:

Tasks:

Key People:

Arena:

Vision:

Due Date:

Big Rocks:

Tasks:

Key People:

Arena:

Vision:

Due Date:

Big Rocks:

Tasks:

Key People:

THE BLUEPRINT

Arena:

Vision:

Due Date:

Big Rocks:

Tasks:

Key People:

Arena:

Vision:

Due Date:

Big Rocks:

Tasks:

Key People:

Arena:

Vision:

Due Date:

Big Rocks:

Tasks:

Key People:

PART 2

Proven Success Principles

For over 40 years the principles outlined in this section have been the common threads in all the successes of the 2,000 plus clients of Mr. Fannin. These principles have met the test of time and have been literally transported around the world.

CHAPTER 10

Protect Your Greatest Asset

Now that your Blueprint is set (although you can change it at any time), you are now ready to manage the thoughts within each Life Arena. With 2,000 to 3,000 thoughts per day they will not be divided evenly.

The good news: Some of your daily thoughts can reach your subconscious, remain there, and positively influence your actions and results.

The bad news: Some of your daily thoughts can reach your subconscious, remain there, and negatively influence your actions and results.

Your subconscious mind is your greatest asset.

Programming or reprogramming this internal wisdom machine, which governs all of your actions, is your key to success. Protecting this asset from unwanted images is your sole responsibility. Mom cannot help you here. However, with **FREE Will** (your greatest gift), you have the authority to facilitate change.

There are two types of people.

Why does one person have success after success, and another has challenges just meeting daily standards? Why do people similar in style, talent, and opportunity have wide discrepancies in results? There are two types of people. One is energized with confidence and faith. He or she sees possibilities for success everywhere. He "knows" that he is born to win and succeed. She "knows" good fortune favors the bold. In fact, he believes, "I am the luckiest man in the world." Calculated risk brings out the best in this person.

Then there is the type of person that is de-energized. He or she has fears and doubts. Not necessarily doubts or fears of reaching mediocrity, but low energy for reaching maximum performance potential. This person thinks problems. He fears risk and avoids confrontation. What is the secret that one person possesses that sets him or her apart from their contemporaries?

The secret to one's success lies in the power found in the subconscious mind, the computer mainframe for infinite intelligence. This mind governs, controls, and directs your life. And yes...you have conscious free will to protect it from negative influence and nurture it for your positive gain.

Your subconscious mind works behind the scenes like the Wizard of Oz. As your greatest asset, it is pulling the strings of your successes. Unfortunately, it can conjure up your failures just as easily. It is amenable to suggestion. Whatever you impress on your subconscious will be expressed on the screen of space as events, conditions, or experiences. "Garbage in, garbage out!" Plant positive seeds of thought and you will reap a bountiful harvest. Plant negative seeds and you may rue the day.

Check the suggestions that people give to you. You will find that many of these suggestions are for the purpose of making you think, feel, and act as THEY want and in ways that are to their advantage. This is manipulation and it should not be allowed. Study what is said. Much is propaganda. Many statements said to you are based on false assumptions, hearsay, or gossip. Some examples are:

- ▶ You need luck to do that!
- ▶ You haven't got a chance.
- ▶ It's no use.
- ▶ It's not what you know, but whom you know.
- ▶ You're too old.
- ▶ We can't win for losing.
- ▶ You can't trust a soul.
- ▶ The world's all screwed up.
- ▶ What's the world coming to?
- ▶ Life's an endless grind.
- ▶ You'll never amount to anything
- ▶ That's just the way you are.
- ▶ Love is for the birds.
- ▶ Watch out, you'll get the flu.
- ▶ Everybody's getting sick.
- ▶ It's all about the law of averages.
- ▶ If we had better direction, we would perform better.
- ▶ They don't care what we do.
- ▶ We just need to do our jobs and keep our mouths shut.

DO NOT INITIATE OR PASS ALONG
THESE TYPES OF STATEMENTS

You control what goes into your subconscious. You are the master filter. You have to give your mental consent. Other people's thoughts must become yours for them to be an action in your mind. If the words are not to your liking, dismiss them or replace them with what's best for you. You are the conscious sentry that protects your greatest asset.

Once your subconscious mind accepts an idea or thought, it begins to execute it. You will always receive a reaction or response from your subconscious mind according to the nature of the thought in your conscious mind.

Your subconscious does not reason or think things out. It does not argue. It does not make comparisons or contrasts. It is like the soil that accepts any kind of seed, good or bad. This physical computer doesn't know or care whether your thoughts are good or bad, true or false or right or wrong.

Remember! Whatever your subconscious believes and expects, it will manifest into its physical equivalent. Thoughts of despair and money woes will keep you in poverty. Thoughts of prosperity will lead to wealth and abundance. Which Arena contains negative thoughts? Stand guard and protect your greatest possession, your subconscious mind.

CHAPTER 11

Think About What
You Think About

Your conscious thoughts permeate The Blueprint within your Life Arenas. These individual and collective thoughts created The Blueprint. As you move forward to turn your life plan into reality, know the power of each of your thoughts.

Here's an example. You're at work and your mind wanders to your weekend plans. You're going to a barbecue at the home of one of your neighbors that you don't know very well.

"I wonder what it will be like? What kind of food will they have? Should I bring something? If so, what? I wonder if that guy Joe will be there? We had that conflict last year over his dog. I hope he's not there, and if he is, I hope he's not a jerk. Speaking of jerks, I better get to that meeting with my boss."

Each of your thoughts is typically twelve to fourteen seconds in duration. Thoughts are about the past, future, or present. Every thought you possess in a day can be measured on a machine in the hospital called an encephalograph. Every thought is an electrical current and this machine measures the electrical current of each thought.

From physics, we know an electrical current is an action and every action has a reaction.

However, a thought is different.

Each thought has three simultaneous reactions.

The first reaction to your thought is **physical**. Think of something sad. Instantly, you will have a physical reaction to this thought. Anybody in the room can see that your head is down, you have a frown (definitely not a smile), and there's sadness reflected from your eyes. Every thought you have has a physical reaction and most people can see it.

If you're thinking about something in the future, you'll look up to your right where creativity is housed. If you're thinking about something that occurred in the past, you'll look up to the left where your memory of images is housed.

If you're trying to think about what someone said, you'll look straight across to the left, because that's where your memory of sound or what someone has said is housed. If you're trying to project what someone's going to say and you're thinking about it, you'll look straight across to your right.

75

Every thought has a physical reaction.

Can you mask the physical reaction to your thoughts? Some of the best poker players in the world (many of my clients) have been studied and the answer is "yes." You can absolutely mask the physical reaction to your thoughts. But there's a second simultaneous reaction to your thoughts. This one's tougher to mask. It's the **emotional** reaction to your thoughts.

When you had the sad thought, it triggered a chemical change of your serotonin level and you felt sad.

When you think of something happy, endorphins flow into your blood stream. You may look happy, but now you literally *feel* happy.

Every thought has an emotional reaction.

Most of us are not aware of this action and reaction. We leave our emotions hanging out on our sleeve for everybody to see and read and it's difficult to mask.

There is a third simultaneous reaction to each of your thoughts, one we cannot mask. It's an **intuitive** vibration or vibe and it can be picked up literally by anyone, regardless of geographical distance. Moms are great at intuitively acting upon this reaction for the safety and well-being of their children. "I just had a hunch something was wrong. Are you okay, baby?" your mom asks by phone. You haven't seen your mother in months or spoken in weeks due to living in different countries, but she had a vibe that something was wrong, which prompted her call. Mom received the reaction to your thoughts prompting her to reach out to you.

Every thought has an intuitive reaction.

Every thought has three simultaneous reactions that are readable physically, emotionally and intuitively. The good news is your thoughts are being broadcast. Of course, the bad news is your thoughts are being broadcast.

Most outcomes are decided before the game is played.

It was while coaching at a professional tennis tournament in England that my skill to read the physical, emotional, and intuitive reaction to a player's thoughts elevated to another level. As a traveling coach, I had met every player on the tour. Many tournaments had only thirty-two players in the draw. While in the locker room, I talked to everyone I could. "How are you? How's your ankle? Nice win last week." How each player responded to me with their physical, emotional, and intuitive reaction and how they acted and interacted in the locker room and on the practice courts revealed their innermost thoughts. I quickly became aware of who was going to win and who would lose.

It didn't take long to learn most matches were decided before the match began. With a newfound ability to predict matches, I now knew how my Mom and Dad felt when their only child was off his game. Most parents are observant and aware. Of course, they can recognize the body language, out of control emotion, and internal negative vibes long before the damage is done and the self-awareness of their child finally arrives.

Champions mentally win first, then enter the arena. Others enter the arena, and then try to figure out what to do.

Think about what you think about. The Blueprint with the "Go to Higher Ground" feature allows you to take inventory of what is on your conscious mind. It also allows you to read the thoughts of the Key People within each Arena. Use this reading ability to influence win-win relationships. Know your intentions and act appropriately.

CHAPTER 12

See It, as if It's So

SEE IT, AS IF IT'S SO

It was the summer of 1962 and I was honing my newfound tennis skills on the Central Park courts in Ashland, Kentucky. It was a hot day and I was sitting on a park bench reading a monthly international tennis magazine. I was particularly interested in an article about two Italian boys (both of whom were my age of twelve) who had been playing the European junior tennis circuit.

As I turned the page, my mentor (Professor R.W. Ross) walked behind me and said, "You could go there." I looked up and smiled.

"What do you mean, Professor?" I asked.

He replied, "See it in your mind's eye. Play tennis with them. Travel with them. Shut your eyes and see it as if it's so."

The next day the same scenario played out. As I reread the article about these two young Italians, the Professor said, "Go in your mind with them. Travel with them. See yourself playing and winning with them on the world tennis circuit." Again, I looked up and smiled.

The magazine article was never discussed again with the Professor. I can't tell you I envisioned this suggested scenario every night that hot summer, but I saw it in my mind hundreds of times. Those vivid images of two young Italian tennis players stayed with me for many years.

I followed their progress in the newspapers and magazines. Two young boys, my age, living a life I could only dream.

Sixteen years later, our paths finally crossed. In 1978, I coached **Adriano Panatta** and **Paolo Bertolucci** and their Italian Davis Cup Team to the World Finals. We traveled the world together. Thanks Professor. Dreams do come true.

Here's another example. Client **Tony Walker** became the new National Sales Manager of Diamond Resorts International and had a concrete Vision of his future. As I was writing this chapter, he called to inform me how his Blueprint had manifested. Four years earlier, he devised his five-year Blueprint after one of our seminars. He not only achieved and exceeded his Visions and Big Rocks, he accomplished all of them in four years instead of five. Tony was proud to convey, "Every night for four years I visualized my Visions being actualized. I saw each of them as if they were so and how they would be."

Awesome, Tony! You are a true champion.

Visualization is the most powerful tool for positive change. It can help program or reprogram your greatest asset...your subconscious mind. All of my personal clients over the past forty-plus years have used this tool to flesh out their Blueprints and achieve their desired Visions and Big Rocks. Visualization also enabled them to discover new possibilities.

Visualization is your most powerful tool for positive change.

Visualization has been effectively used for thousands of years to create cities, states, and countries. It has helped destroy them as well. It has launched businesses, schools, and charitable organizations. It created the technical rise of the Blackberry phone and it fostered Blackberry's demise.

In a private golf and business retreat at a tony New Jersey golf club, I listened to and observed Blackberry executives talk about their business and industry. It was obvious that they were thinking more about their problems than their solutions. "We have a lot of technical problems. Plus the competition is advancing swiftly and we are losing ground," I heard them say. I believe negative thinking about what they didn't want was dragging the company's overall performance and it squelched any and all imagination and creativity for a positive future.

Visualization has helped amass personal fortune and it's financially ruined many people, including the wealthy. Like a double-edged sword, it can cut both ways.

Approximately fifty percent of your waking hours is spent visualizing or daydreaming. If you sleep eight hours per night, you are awake 112 hours per week. That's 56 hours of visualization! Is your visualization proactive or reactive? Most people visualize as a reaction to their environment with its corresponding circumstances, conditions, and situations. "I hate my job." "What do I do with these bills?" Proactive visualization is the mark of the champion in life, business and sports. "I'm a closer!" "I am accurate." "I am healthy." "I am successful." These are a champion's proactive thoughts.

We imagine what we want and what we don't want in our lives. Most of our thoughts are about challenges we have that we haven't given up on. Each thought places an image on the screen of space in our mind's eye.

How do you see your daydreams?

Most of us see mental images as if we are looking through our own eyes. We see, feel, smell, taste, and hear what's played on our mental screen. Approximately eighty-three percent of humanity visualizes this way. Approximately fifteen percent visualize like they are looking down from above (typically from the right) onto a movie set. And approximately two percent report they see nothing in their mind's eye. In reality, all three methods of visualization work for you (even the one where you see nothing). In all three forms of visualization, your subconscious mind picks up what is there and stores it.

Why is visualization so powerful? Visualization works because your subconscious mind does NOT know the difference between fantasy and reality. (Please memorize this phrase.)

Your subconscious mind does NOT know the difference between fantasy and reality.

This is how a nightmare occurs. Of course, there is no monster in your bedroom while you are asleep. However, your subconscious mind doesn't know this. Since it controls all of your bodily functions, it doesn't realize it is a fantasy and it reacts as if it is happening. Therefore, it reacts to the monster chasing you and your body begins to perspire, your heart races, your breathing becomes labored, your mouth gets dry, and you are finally startled awake. With a jolt you spring out of bed with the hairs on your arms on alert and a sense of foreboding that scares you. It seems so real. After looking under the bed and carefully opening the closet door, you realize it was only a dream. Yes...it bears repeating...

Your subconscious mind does NOT know the difference between fantasy and reality.

How does visualization help success? How can it get in the way? Your subconscious sits in your mind like a person watching a plasma screen 24/7. It controls all bodily functions and it never takes its eye off the screen. If you have a thought of losing weight, the picture on the screen can be the image of an overweight person. "I can't get in these jeans" or "I need to lose weight" are examples. It's not the words, but the image that matters. And the subconscious takes things literally. So, your subconscious saw a fat person in those jeans. Even though you want to lose weight, your subconscious must be true to what it believes and the fat person (you) finally gets another chocolate donut. Scary, isn't it?

Whatever is repeated on the screen of space in your mind, the subconscious responds by creating internal stress, and this activates the body to create or manifest the image into its physical equivalent. Yikes! That's the good news. That's also the bad news. So...what do you do?

Before visualizing, sequester yourself in a quiet place and clear your mind. Unhinge your jaw, shut your eyes, and visualize a blank or dark screen in your mind. There are no thoughts of the past or future. Just be present with the absence of thought. Focus on reducing your breathing from the normal fifteen to seventeen breaths per minute to the champion's breath of six to eight breaths per minute. Do not force this. Take long inhales and long exhales as your body responds. Within seconds, you will feel your shoulders relax. You are now on your way to a mindset that will be receptive to suggestion. Let visualization begin.

Four Types of Visualizations

There are four types of visualizations to assist you in turning your dreams into reality. They are:

1. Task: This is visualizing the same task over and over, such as making a ten-foot birdie putt. I use this daily in my coaching for life, business and sports. Each night, a professional golfer mentally hits ten shots solid with all fourteen clubs in his or her bag. He or she sees and feels the swing striking the ball solidly to a well-defined target. Each night, a tennis player does the same, hitting well-placed serves over and over in his or her mind. A sales person envisions his or her presentation opening over and over before entering any office.

2. Situational: This is the same as Task Visualization, but the ten-foot birdie putt is on the last hole of the Masters with victory riding on your next move. This form of imagery is used with all my clients to prepare for specific conditions, situations, and circumstances. The Illinois men's golf team members visualize each shot they will produce on the course the next day the night before their tournament rounds. This nightly tournament ritual before rounds has produced two NCAA champions and eight Big 10 titles.

Here's another example. MLB pitcher **Dillon Gee** picked off LA Dodger **Carl Crawford** on first base. He had visualized this tactical move two days prior and it was the first time he had ever envisioned it. He texted me after the game, "WOW! How cool was that?"

3. Symbolic: This type of visualization is extremely powerful! It deploys creativity where there are no rules. I have used it to eradicate cancer from my body by creating an imaginary Pac-Man character to eat the cancer cells. This technique has been used to lose weight, make money, and manifest a zillion other accomplishments. This tool for wellness, as well as success in business and sport, has worked with all my clients.

4. Aftermath: This form of visualization is seldom utilized (even by the superstars). Athletes **Mike Tyson, Terrell Owens, Randy Moss,** and **Lance Armstrong,** as well as former San Diego mayor **Bob Filner,** former Toronto mayor **Rob Ford,** and others who have been at the pinnacle of success could have benefitted from this effective tool. Each failed to see what happens after the fame and fortune have arrived. All of my clients are aware of Aftermath Visualization and ninety-nine percent have used it wisely. However, a few laid this tool off to the side, much to my chagrin.

Reaching the pinnacle of success is one thing. Staying there is a completely different paradigm.

Preparing how their family, friends, associates, colleagues, competitors, and fans would react to their success was the missing link for the myriad success stories that eventually turned to failure. Most never saw it coming.

Your visualization has dictated who you are today.

It's time to be proactive. You're going to visualize half of your waking hours anyway. You might as well envision The Blueprint turning into reality with the power of positive visualization.

See it, as if it's so. See it, as it will be.

Visualization 101

Find a quiet place to visualize. Have zero distractions. Relax by lowering your breathing to six to eight breaths per minute. Observe the picture of the yacht below. Now shut your eyes and keep this image in your mind's eye. If and when you lose the image, open your eyes and repeat the process. Eventually you will be able to hold this image for longer periods.

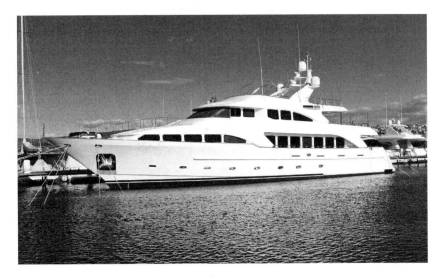

Next…see the image and place it in your mind again. Relax. Shut your eyes. This time, start the engine and hear the yacht prepare to sail. Now create a video of the craft moving away from its dock. The more you can add sound, color, movement, smell, taste, and touch to your Visions, the more amenable your subconscious will be to receiving this image.

Your Vision Board

Get relaxed. Close your eyes. Envision each of your Life Arenas. Mentally picture the Vision for each Arena in a completed, finished state. See it, as if it's so. See it in your mind, as it will be.

This is a simple Vision Board. There are (intentionally) no Big Rocks or Tasks. I strongly recommend going weekly (at a minimum) to Higher Ground. Visualizing before bedtime is especially recommended for visualizing your Primary Arena. This Vision tucks you in bed at night and wakes you up in the morning.

Arena:
Vision:

Arena:
Vision:

Arena:
Vision:

Arena:
Vision:

Arena:
Vision:

Arena:
Vision:

Arena:
Vision:

Arena:
Vision:

Arena:
Vision:

Arena:
Vision:

CHAPTER 13

The Russian Dolls™

While delivering seminars in the Ukraine in the late 1980s, I came across a set of Russian nesting dolls on a shopping trip in Kiev. Upon inspecting my new purchase of seven dolls, each was stacked within the next larger doll. Made from wood and placed on a lathe, each doll was crafted and hand painted with vibrant colors and a unique design. The first doll depicted the mother. This was the largest doll and it represented the master or the boss. The remaining dolls were inside one another until the final, smallest doll (designed as a baby) was alone on the table. Within seconds of placing all the dolls on the table, **synchronized visualization**™ was born in me.

The concept of the Russian Dolls™ can help you ensure that you reach each Vision and turn The Blueprint into reality by synchronizing your proactive visualizations in the following time sequence:

Single Performance

Visualize opening and closing any performance where it's important to attract the Zone. Never have a physical workout without mentally rehearsing. Mentally preview each of your meetings, practices, conferences, appointments and encounters. Picture the outcome desired once this single performance is complete.

These individual performances are to be thread into the day, week, month, quarter and year.

Daily

Never have a day you haven't already had. Each night, take ninety-seconds to visualize your next day on earth as the greatest day possible. See it with the Big Rocks intact.

Each day is 1/7 of a great week and 1/30 of an awesome month. Thread the day into the next week, month, quarter, and year.

Daily Mental Rehearsal

(Utilize the night before each day)

The Daily Mental Rehearsal is written in a daily task list format to coincide with your Blueprint.

TOMORROW: _____ DATE: _____

At the end of each day, list the tasks to be accomplished for the next day. Give a mental rehearsal for each future task. The next morning, briefly scan your list. Proceed with action.

At the conclusion of the day, throw this list away. Begin a new list. Give a mental rehearsal for each task. Repeat this process daily.

If any task is written three days in a row do ONE of the following:

1. Delete the task entirely.
2. Delegate or transfer the task to someone else.
3. DO THE TASK IMMEDIATELY WITHOUT FURTHER PROCRASTINATION.

Tomorrow's List

1.

2.

3.

4.

5.

Weekly

On Sunday night, tens of thousands of Zoniacs™ take some "alone time" and visualize their greatest week ever. Know what you would like to accomplish each week. As $\frac{1}{52}$ of your greatest year ever, it's crucial to chip away at your Visions and Big Rocks. Know how the week fits snugly into your upcoming month, quarter, and year.

Always envision each upcoming week.

Monthly

One month can peel off your calendar easily. However, you can accomplish a lot in this 28- to 31-day period. What Big Rocks will be completed once this upcoming month is complete? How does $\frac{1}{12}$ of your year impact your Annual Vision? Never have a month you haven't already had.

On the last day of each month, spend a little time alone and plan your greatest month ever.

Always envision each upcoming month.

Quarterly

There are obviously four quarters in every year. Challenge yourself each upcoming quarter. You can accomplish a lot in three months. Each quarter has inherent challenges. The first quarter of January, February, and March launches your year. This quarter sets the tone. With renewed vigor and an annual plan, start this quarter focused and with purpose.

The second quarter of April, May, and June reveals golf season, end of the school year, and the beginning of summer. Prepare accordingly.

The third quarter of July, August, and September has golf, tennis, swimming, summer vacations, and back-to-school preparations. With half of your year off the calendar you may need to reinvent your year or adjust your Big Rocks, Strategies, and Tactics.

Champions love the fourth quarter. These ninety-two days are a time to finalize your annual plans. This quarter also has major distractions such as Thanksgiving, Christmas and other holidays, and New Year's Eve. The fourth quarter is also a time to prepare for your next year.

Always envision each upcoming quarter.

Annually

Every New Year's Eve, tens of thousands of Zoniacs™ spend a little time alone. Each visualizes one year in advance to next year's December 31. Mentally they raise a symbolic toast to celebrate the greatest year of their lives. Then it must be asked, "What do I need to accomplish to make this so?" Whatever you choose, this becomes the mother of all your yearly actions. Every performance, day, week, month, and quarter fit together like the Russian Dolls™.

The Russian Dolls™ Is Synchronized Visualization™

The application of each of these scheduled visualizations takes very little time. Your annual visualization needs your utmost due diligence and well-thought out time. After your Vision for your Primary Arena is set, the other Russian Dolls™ take no more than ninety-seconds.

The Russian Dolls™ concept has worked for all my clients and it continues to bring results for all that wield its power.

CHAPTER 14

The Amazing Zone

By major league baseball standards, **Sean Bergman** was a mediocre player. His up and down performances were due to his up and down mindset. With his wife anxious to start a family, he felt tremendous pressure to succeed and he knew that the window of opportunity in professional baseball was small. With an unfortunate injury he also knew his career could instantly be over. Attracting the Zone on a daily basis was the answer.

Although **Sean Bergman** had been locked in the mindset where peak performance resides (that's how he reached the big leagues), the day-in and day-out Zone had eluded him. This professional athlete started putting the Zone on like an overcoat every day. Remarkably, when he made this mental paradigm shift to extreme positivity, the defense of his **Houston Astros** teammates picked up when he took the mound. Mentally, he sparked a collective team tsunami that produced fifteen victories. "Being able to attract the Zone at will changed my career and ultimately my life," reflects Bergman. The results tripled his income and set him up for long-term retirement.

The Zone phenomenon resides in all of us. This mind-body fusion of peak performance is NOT just for the superstar athlete. Being in this productive mindset can be achieved in every Life Arena within The Blueprint. Everyone, regardless of age, experience, or talent, can attract this "purposeful calm" feeling where everything seems possible. Because your best always surfaces when in the Zone, it's the only place to be.

Can you attract the Zone in every Life Arena?

Absolutely. You can be in the Zone when you parent. You can be locked-in to this peak performance state of mind and body when you are interacting with your "significant other." In fact, you can be in or near the Zone in all you do. Period.

THE ZONE: WHAT HAPPENS IN YOUR BODY

EYES
Your eyes create the illusion that everything happens in slow motion. In a crisis, this is so you can look for an avenue of escape, or fight off an adversary.

MIND
Your conscious mind shuts down; your intuition takes over.

JAW
Your jaw unclenches; which is why Michael Jordan's tongue would hang out at the end of close playoff games.

HEART
Your heart rate quickens.

LUNGS
Your breathing slows.

BLOOD
Blood gets dirverted to your brain and to the large muscles; this gives you mental clarity, as well as inordinate speed, strength, balance, and agility.

SKIN
Your skin sensitivity heightens.

What happens to your mind and body?

EYES
Your eyes create the illusion that everything is in slow motion. In a crisis, this is so you can look for an avenue of escape or rescue and or fend off an adversary or threatening challenge.

HEART
Your heart rate quickens.

DIGESTION
Your digestive system slows down and can even shut down.

THE BLUEPRINT

BLOOD
Blood is diverted from your stomach to your brain for clarity and the large muscles for inordinate strength, speed, quickness, balance, and agility.

IMMUNE SYSTEM
Your immune system goes on full alert.

SELF-HEALING
The body is fully prepared for instant super-healing.

MIND
Your conscious mind shuts down regarding your future and past and it locks in on the immediate task at hand. Intuition emanating from your subconscious mind ultimately takes over, as it scours the environment 360° for immediate challenges. With this information, it swiftly calculates your next move. Creativity is maximized. Memory for the task at hand is fully activated for easy and relevant access.

JAW
Your jaw unclenches so the body can relax and be subordinate to the subconscious mind.

LUNGS
Breathing slows to approximately six to eight breaths per minute. The volumes of your inhales and exhales increase providing ready oxygen to maximize short bursts of physical movement. Enhanced endurance is swiftly activated for long-term challenges.

SKIN
Skin sensitivity is heightened. Physical sensors are activated for recognizing potential threats to your safety. This information is also utilized for assessing the situation, condition, and circumstance as you actively pursue your goals.

MUSCLES
Your muscles become fully activated for more strength, speed, agility, and quickness. In addition, they are synchronized for efficiency, fluidity, and smoothness. The instant coordination of your muscles produces extraordinary physical results.

FEELINGS

You will have a feeling of a "purposeful calm" where nothing can go wrong. Confidence will soar while your relaxation will keep you away from panic and the sense of peril, doom, and despair. You feel tremendous energy and power. A feeling of well-being blankets you and gives you a sense that anything is possible.

What are the Zone attributes?

▸ Perform your physical workouts with more strength, speed, agility, quickness, and endurance.
▸ Study better and longer with enhanced retention.
▸ Improve creativity in general, specifically in writing, speaking, music, and dance.
▸ Make better, faster decisions.
▸ Enhance your ability to excel while taking tests, quizzes, and exams under pressure.
▸ Perform under pressure in sports with your best mental, physical, and technical peak performance.
▸ Attract like-minded peak performers and achievers or Zoniacs™ (individuals who intentionally attract the Zone).
▸ Manage your days with little to no worries, hassles, anxiety, or negativity.
▸ Be able to easily read the three reactions to another person's thoughts (physical, emotional, and intuitive).
▸ Expand your ability to focus in the present tense.
▸ Know intuitively the next move of your team or competition.
▸ Possess super healing capacity by accelerating recovery from injury, illness, and/or disease.
▸ Activate and enhance your immune system, thus preventing disease and or sickness.
▸ Sell products and or services more effectively and consistently.
▸ Bolster your overall physical and mental energy.
▸ Possess more confidence in ALL you do.
▸ Simplify and balance ALL aspects of life.
▸ Lead other people more effectively.
▸ Enhance your mental and physical presence in a group.

- ▶ Activate an uncanny sense of knowing.
- ▶ Allows you NOT to sweat the small stuff in life.
- ▶ Attract your life, business, and sports Visions and Big Rocks more readily and easily.
- ▶ Activate better and more productive teamwork.
- ▶ Ignite the passion in your relationships.

Why the Zone?

Because it's in you right now! The Zone phenomenon is attainable by everyone. Its physical design has been passed from generation to generation into your DNA. With the ability to effectively respond to trauma, stress, pressure, and the overall hassles of life, you can now live with simplicity, balance, and excellence. As a consistent Zone performer or Zoniac® you can accomplish all of your goals and dreams. Why not?

How do I attract the Zone?

The S.C.O.R.E.® Success System (Chapter 15) with its myriad tools (including the Russian Dolls™) is the ONLY proven formula for attracting the Zone. The attributes of living and performing in this mindset will give you an edge in ALL you do. All you need is an investment of three percent (or less) of your waking hours to apply S.C.O.R.E.®

Why are you waiting? Attract the Zone!

Most of us have played sports in some form or another. Some of us were good and others were mediocre. The majority who played youth sports experienced a phenomenon that showed up once or multiple times during their participation. It was the experience of the Zone. Here you felt empowered. Your focus was laser-like. Your confidence soared. Your intuition was uncanny. You were relaxed. And the passion and enthusiasm that ran through your veins uplifted you. With purpose and calm you performed like never before. Remember? After leaving the sports arena, you still kept an eye on the game. As a spectator, you watch the elite on your favorite team strive to gain an edge over the competition. You love watching their Zone performances. It's here that the games become memorable. This is why you watch. This was why you played. What can the Zone do for you now?

The Zone overcomes adversity.

The Zone found its way into **Jesse Owens** as a young college sprinter in May 1934. Owens had injured his back when performing antics with a fraternity brother shortly before the Big 10 Track & Field Championships. On the day of the event, he woke from his heating pads so stiff that his teammates had to help him into the seat of his coach's car.

With his coach, **Larry Snyder**, ready to scratch him from the Championships, Owens said, "I'd like to try at least the 100." As he prepared to run, his back began hurting as he dug his feet into the ground at the starting mark. Owens allegedly commented, "When the starter said 'set,' there suddenly was no more pain."

He won the race in 9.4 seconds, tying the world record. He went on to break world records in the long jump, the 200-yard dash, and the 220-yard low hurdles. Some say this is the world's greatest sports accomplishment. How could a man propel himself to such great feats when his injury would have kept most athletes from competing?

By attracting the Zone, you can overcome illness, disease, and injury. The chemicals that flow through your body while in a Zone state have super-healing properties. The athletes I coach get back on the field twenty-five to fifty percent quicker than their trainers or doctors projected. In fact, by attracting the Zone for thirty days in a row, I tapped into super-healing by defeating skin cancer with no medications or cancer treatments.

The Zone erases old paradigms.

A client chased his dream of winning the yearlong hunt of holding the prize for the best race car driver in his class. For fourteen years, he toiled and secured second place, but missed the coveted top prize. He choked. He tried too hard. He got nervous. He lost passion. He drove with doubt. Over a decade of negative thinking, he had thought, "I just can't catch a break." But not now!

First, he updated his Life Blueprint and convinced himself he was a champion. He committed to turning his Racing Arena's Visions and Big

Rocks into reality. "I am a champion" was his renewed mantra. He changed all his mental routines. "Every race I had specific routines to attract the Zone. I never wavered regardless of how I finished the race," he bluntly stated. He made adjustments swiftly during the races. He treated winning and losing the same as he evaluated without emotion. And he attracted the Zone every weekend for every race this particular season.

Going into the last race with the S.C.O.R.E.® Success System riding shotgun, he overcame an eight-point deficit. He drove in the Zone! At last, the perennial champion was dethroned and the losing paradigm was erased. "The Zone conquers all!" racecar champion **Chad Sellers** exclaimed.

I was mentally with this client the entire racing season. He was in the Zone at every turn. He erased the past, one lap at a time. By season's end, he was not the same driver as before. He starved the victim and the judge and only fed the champion. I am so proud of his Zone accomplishments. What an ending to a decade-long quest!

The Zone takes you to unthinkable, great heights.

Frank Thomas is a big man. At 6'5" and 250 pounds, he is larger than life. Before the 1997 baseball season, the "Big Hurt" set the batting title in his sights as the season's main Big Rock. Conventional wisdom said that a man that size could not possibly win the batting crown. Most felt Frank would have few, if any, infield hits and bunting for a hit was not an option. A batting title was unthinkable. Frank believed, "If I take some walks and become very selective at the plate, I can do this. When I attract the Zone every game, my vision will become reality."

Winning the American League batting title with a .347 average was Frank's greatest accomplishment. Winning a batting title for a man his size was a formidable task, but when he put his mind to it, I knew it would get done. In addition, Frank knocked out 35 home runs and drove in 125 runs. The Zone took him to great heights.

The Zone is achievable in any life endeavor by anyone.

A Calgary client's life was in a tailspin. She was depressed over her career, body weight, and taking care of her son. She began a daily Zone regimen and her confidence began to soar. She swiftly changed her thoughts. She set new goals and decided to take charge of her life. No more medications. No more pity parties. No more being a victim. She woke up and completely reinvented herself. She dropped sixty pounds without the help of a gym or diet center. Now her Life Arenas of career, self, parent, friend, and finance are simple and balanced.

When she called our offices, she was in a negative place. Her turn-around is remarkable. She deserves all that life can offer. She is now physically fit, a great mom, and a very smart businesswoman. Kudos to her! The sky is the limit with her customized Zone formula.

The Zone brings simplicity and balance.

Chris Williams had a business life that was complicated. His industry profit margins were getting thinner. Stress, from the accountability and responsibility from the job, was being taken home. He gave less attention to his family. He quit taking care of himself physically. And then he began a ninety-day transformation that completely overhauled his thirty-year old business model. He attracted the Zone in all of his life arenas. He carved out time to think. Stress didn't completely leave his desk, but it was sliced by at least eighty percent. A new perspective arrived. And by viewing his life objectively from Higher Ground, simplicity and balance became his norm. His business is now tracking hundred-fold profits and he's in control of his life.

Over two decades ago, I had coached Chris to the Illinois State High School Tennis Finals. He was a champion! And then our paths went in different directions until decades later. Although he was still a champion, he was not getting in the Zone in business or life on a daily basis. His perseverance and tenacity paid off in just ninety-days. Great job Chris! You now have the life you deserve.

The Zone will help your golf game.

The next day following a three-hour S.C.O.R.E.® Workshop, **Philip Slowik** shot a 64 at the Medina Country Club, setting the course record. His previous best round of golf was a 72. The next week, he won the Illinois State Junior Open and received a college scholarship. The Zone worked magic for him.

Since 1971, I witnessed miraculous accomplishments after applying the S.C.O.R.E. *Success System. A twenty-four-hour turnaround is possible, although it depends on the individual. After helping ten golfers (and counting) win their first professional tournament, I know S.C.O.R.E.* *golf tools will attract the Zone and instantly work.*

The Zone will save your marriage.

Marriage is an area of life where the Zone seldom gets credit. Two people meet with a shared vision. Two people marry. Two people raise a family. Two people have different careers. Finances get strained. Stress enters the bedroom, kitchen, den, and finally the whole house. Then the two people wake up for whatever reason and say, "Who are you?" Yes, marriage can get complicated. When the Zone finds a marriage partnership, the passion immediately returns. Mutual daily respect is heightened. The "I please you" attitude is set in motion. Shared vision is reconnected. And two people live happily ever after. The end.

In the summer of 2014, I conducted a small seminar full of men. Eight egos with visions of great success were in my leadership workshop. The results, after learning about the S.C.O.R.E. *Success System and the 90-Second Rule™, were amazing!*

Six of the men were having marital issues and were contem-plating divorce. I'm proud to say that five of the men reconciled and married life has never been better. The sixth husband is still work-ing on it. All are better leaders and making more money.

The Zone is attainable by everyone at any time and place. It's in *you* right now! Tapping into this amazing power source is simple and easy. But first you must believe this mindset exists. To attract the power of the Zone, try my simple formula of the S.C.O.R.E.* Success System.

It just works! Using it daily will attract the Zone where a "purposeful calm" feeling will engulf you. Here your talents will be leveraged and your dreams will be realized.

The S.C.O.R.E.˚ Success System is ready to fuel your Visions. With it, you WILL attract the Zone. Go to the next chapter and receive this compass that will keep you on course until your dream is a reality.

S.C.O.R.E.®

SUCCESS SYSTEM

CHAPTER 15

S.C.O.R.E.® Success System

Where's the compass for staying on course and in the Zone? In 1974, during an eighteen-month, independent research project with over 250 children ages four to eight years old participating, the answer was revealed to the question, "How do we facilitate super learning in children?" It was here that five performance markers or components were discovered that all humans possess. They are:

Self-discipline • Concentration • Optimism
Relaxation • Enjoyment

Each of these markers triggers natural chemicals in the mind and body that can collectively unleash the powerful Zone phenomenon. When these intangible markers are balanced at a high level, a chemical cocktail of cortisol, glycogen, adrenalin, dopamine, serotonin, endorphins, and so forth, is naturally fuel-injected into the bloodstream. The "purposeful calm" feeling of the Zone arrives and its attributes are simultaneously released. Welcome peak performance!

The collection of these five markers forms the acronym S.C.O.R.E.® and it's this domino-like chain that reflects your overall attitude at any given time. All of your daily thoughts are contained within these five intangibles. Therefore:

Your attitude and overall S.C.O.R.E.® level are the same.

S.C.O.R.E.® has been the common denominator for millions of athletes, business executives, and everyday people. It has never wavered in its uncanny ability to be the over-arching compass guide for turning The Blueprint into reality. Designed to withstand the most intense pressures of life, this unique and simple thought management system can be learned and applied swiftly. It can be customized to your personality and strengths and it is adaptable to any aspect of your life, business, or sport.

Everyone, regardless of age, economic or social status, nationality, race, or sex has a high or low level of S.C.O.R.E.® at any given time.

Once you become aware of these five intangibles in your life, you will be able to plan your performances with assuredness that you will prevail. Even though you may have performances that aren't going your way, you will be armed with concrete, proven tools and techniques for swift adjustments.

The five markers of S.C.O.R.E.® govern every aspect of your life. Now you can readily take charge of your destiny. In fact, every Life Arena has a collective S.C.O.R.E.® Level consisting of the aggregate S.C.O.R.E.® Levels of you and your Key People.

For example, you can enter your Spouse Arena with a Zone state of mind and just like that you can get ambushed with a catastrophe that your "significant other" brought home from her work. Good-bye Zone.

All Key People within each of your Arenas have a S.C.O.R.E.® Level that can and will fluctuate. One Arena can have high levels of Optimism and in an hour it has plummeted to the most negative level.

Know S.C.O.R.E.® because it impacts ALL you do.

It is recommended that you learn the definitions (in bold) of each S.C.O.R.E.® component. They are:

Self-discipline

This initial component of S.C.O.R.E.® is Self-discipline or "S" and it typically is the stumbling block for most people. The absence of a life, business, or sports Blueprint is usually the culprit. In fact, not one of my 2,500+ clients walked in with a Blueprint tucked under his or her arm asking me to help manifest it into reality.

Self-discipline is the main point of this book. Most people do not have a definitive life vision with corresponding, well-defined goals for every aspect of their life. And if they do, they lack the commitment and know-how to get them through formidable adversity and challenges.

The definition is:

Self-discipline or S is the willingness and commitment while executing well-defined tasks that lead to well-defined goals and ultimately to your Visions.

We all possess a high or low level of Self-discipline, and it can fluctuate wildly for most performers. How is your Self-discipline in all

aspects of your life? You can have high self-discipline as a businessperson and low self-discipline with your physical wellness. You can have ultimate fitness due to your self-discipline and low self-discipline in your "significant other" relationship.

Know, understand, and elevate this integral component in your life and you will be on your way to simplicity, balance, and abundance.

Creating The Blueprint is the first step in bolstering Self-discipline. Congratulations!

High S has jurisdiction over vision, dreams, foresight, goals, strategy, tactics, determination, insistence, intention, diligence, tasks, tolerance, resolution, perseverance, self-control, commitment, dedication, willingness, and purpose.

Low S has jurisdiction over aimlessness, procrastination, impatience, frustration, being lost, chaos, confusion, feeling disordered, jumbled, puzzled, intolerance, annoyed, disoriented, poor time management, tardiness, being disorganized, incompetent, or feeling muddled.

Rate your Self-discipline and the Self-discipline of each of your Arena Key People.

Concentration

Most of my client base has a high IQ. Unfortunately, the higher their IQ, the more difficult it can be to keep them focused. My most creative clients are challenged to corral their thoughts and harness their collective power. Many of these creative types are not finishers or closers.

The less intelligent clients can more readily focus. No names will be offered here. They have learned that concentrated energy is the only way for them to survive and thrive. With less to think about, it becomes easier for them to focus on the task at hand.

Many CEOs of small- to medium-sized companies that I've coached have a concentration challenge. Mix in the Internet with social media intrusion, bombardment from their cellphone, and trying to balance the rest of their life, it's easy to see why concentration has plummeted for most executives over the last decade. Add the overarching need to micromanage their business and it's no wonder there is a struggle.

Most parents have a concentration challenge. We juggle our kids' schedules and our own. As moms and dads, we want to teach our children how to be successful in life. When our children are toddlers, we send them to time-out. Typically we cut the time-out short because they look so pitiful and cute. We lose focus on the whole point of the punishment. We ground them when they mess up as teens and even take away their precious cellphones. With that stated, we also cave-in and short-circuit their punishments. Not my parents.

I learned my greatest concentration lesson as a teenager. I got caught drinking alcohol at the age of fifteen. I was grounded and confined to my room for thirty days. I really felt my warden-like mom and dad would give me early release for good behavior. Day 10 arrived, and I was still under house arrest and there was no reprieve. Day 15 was no better. I pleaded my case to deaf ears on Day 20. Finally on Day 30, I was freed, although still on parole. There was an epic pool party that night and my girlfriend would be looking smashing. I couldn't wait. As I preened in the mirror to go out for the night, my father said, "Where are you going? Thirty days is thirty days. You can go out tomorrow." They focused on my lesson to be learned. What the &*$%, parents? Really? That lesson is still alive over fifty years later. Nice focus, Mom and Dad. Throughout my life you focused on the lessons I needed to learn. I get it now.

Once you become more self-disciplined, you can now narrow your focus and apply Concentration or "C," the second letter in the S.C.O.R.E.® acronym. In order to maximize Concentration, you must have visions, plans, strategies, tactics, objectives, and targets to send your energy. The smaller the goals and targets, the more laser focus will arrive.

The definition is:

Concentration or C is the ability to mentally and physically focus your energy while executing well-defined tasks that lead to well-defined goals and ultimately your Visions.

How long can you maintain your concentration? What causes you to lose focus? How do you swiftly get it back? When you fully apply tools and techniques of the S.C.O.R.E.® Success System, you will possess the answers and apply the solutions.

There are many concrete, proven Concentration or "C" tools to help you increase this S.C.O.R.E.® component. Soon you will be more efficient with more accuracy and quality in your work and play. With a narrowed focus, you will be able to accomplish more in less time.

High C has jurisdiction over quality, focus, attentiveness, tunnel vision, exactness, correctness, meticulousness, resolve, detailed, methodical, thorough, determination, fastidiousness, application, accuracy, precision, and single-mindedness.

Low C has jurisdiction over daydreaming, distraction, inattention, carelessness, negligence, lack of focus, boredom, disruption, mistakenness, imprecision, incompetence, ineffectiveness, inaccuracy, ineptitude, wastefulness, and inefficiency, absent-mindedness, and uselessness.

Rate your Concentration and the Concentration of each of your Arena Key People.

Optimism

Great leaders have swagger. You might not see it, but you can feel it when they're in your presence. They know who they are and understand exactly where they want to go and how to get there. You can see and feel a high-level optimist. When I first met **Mitch Joel,** he was one of many speakers with me on tour in Canada. By coincidence, I was

going to work out before taking the stage around 1:00 p.m. It was early and I had just awakened. Mitch grabbed me by the arm in the hotel lobby. "I need your help. I'm freaked out about my upcoming talk," he pleaded. He was so nervous, as he was due on stage in less than an hour. His confidence was low and his expectations were even lower. He was an expert for sure, but didn't have the experience and the swagger to rock the house. With a few ninety-second tools, Mitch walked away with a relaxed bounce in his step. I rushed my workout to go watch his presentation. Wow! How he changed with only a few tools! He walked on stage a different man than I saw back in the lobby. Today, he exudes optimism as people flock to hear his every word.

Here is **Mitch Joel** today. When Google wants someone to explain the latest developments in marketing to the top brands in the world, they bring Mitch Joel to the Googleplex in Mountain View, California. *Marketing* magazine dubbed him the "Rock Star of Digital Marketing" and called him, "one of North America's leading digital visionaries." Back in 2006, he was named one of the most influential authorities on blog marketing in the world. Mitch Joel is president (although he prefers the title "media hacker") of Mirum—a global digital marketing agency operating in close to 20 countries with more than 2,000 employees. He has been called a marketing and communications visionary, interactive expert, and community leader.

Mitch Joel is an optimist.

Here's another example of a struggling artist with a similar style to the great Pablo Picasso with a little touch of Brazilian and South Beach color. I had purchased a painting of his for $200 and wanted to meet artist **Romero Britto**. When I arrived at his namesake gallery in 1988 in Coconut Grove, Florida, he could not look me in the eye. Deep down he knew he was talented but his mindset of extreme optimism had not arrived with him from Brazil. "I have no idea how to market my paintings," he whispered with no optimism. We struck a coaching and management deal that had us working together for the next three years. We spent many late nights on the phone discussing his future. "I am the best artist in the world," Romero thought as he drifted off to sleep each night.

Today, Romero's art is hanging in some of the greatest museums and art galleries in the world. His work has adorned a Super Bowl, Olympics, and hundreds of walls of the rich and famous. He is an acclaimed international artist and it's his eternal optimism that launched his enormously successful career.

Romero Britto is an optimist.

Optimism or "O" is literally and figuratively at the heart and core of the word S.C.O.R.E.® and the S.C.O.R.E.® Success System itself. This is your belief system. It is the glue that holds you together when confronted with challenges that may appear overwhelming. It catapults the good to great and the great to iconic mastery.

From the S.C.O.R.E.® System's powerful 90-Second Rule™ Toolbox, you'll find easy to use tools that will send your confidence soaring. Champions have escalated their Optimism level to their highest. Why not you?

The definition is:

Optimism or O is the belief, expectancy and knowing while executing well-defined tasks that lead to well-defined goals and ultimately your Visions.

Do you have optimism in every aspect of your life? Optimism can and will take you out of your comfort zone and escalate you into the peak performance state of the Zone. Increased optimism is a game-changer. With more confidence, you will more readily expand your horizons with a "go for it" attitude.

High O has jurisdiction over trust, hope, confidence, pride, self-esteem, belief, certainty, expectancy, self-respect, faith, self-worth, conviction, assurance, willpower, self-assurance, and a sense of knowing.

Low O has jurisdiction over pessimism, distrust, doubt, gloom, fear, negativity, cynicism, uncertainty, reservation, hesitation, skepticism, disbelief, hopelessness, impossibility, futility, bleakness, desperateness, negativity, fatalism, low self-esteem, low self-worth, and low self-respect, among other undesirable traits.

Rate your Optimism and the Optimism of each of your Arena Key People.

Relaxation

My PGA golf client couldn't sleep through the night. Two or three times he would awake in a panic. What was happening to him? Going to sleep was a challenge and this fact wreaked havoc on his psyche. Finally, at 2:30 a.m., pro golfer **Doug Barron** called and I was on the phone with him most of the night. "I'm going to withdraw. I can't play," he stated with trepidation.

With no sleep, Doug finally walked onto the first tee box to begin his round. There, he greeted his playing partner for the day, the world's #1 Tiger Woods. Armed with relaxation tools, Doug kept his cool and his mind remained on the task at hand. When he walked off the 18th green, he signed his card with a sensational 68, besting the world's best player. This is one of the greatest feats in golf that no one knows about.

Relaxation challenges have confronted most of my clients. There is a call for help from every corner of the world most nights. Even more than business or sports, we are in a "Relaxation" crisis in all facets of life. We placate ourselves with alcohol and drugs just to chill out and escape the daily grind of existence. You can feel it. You can see it.

One of my clients is the **Kentucky Health Department Association** that represents more than 4.4 million residents. After a two-day seminar, one of the county department heads called for some customized advice. From a place of uncertainty and confusion she said on the phone, "What can we do to reverse the heroin use in our county? Our local high school has over thirty-five percent of its students that have tried this addictive drug." My heart instantly filled with sadness and this revelation from my home state stunned me. In fact, every Kentucky health department representing 120 counties lists heroin as the #1 challenge. Coping with stress and pain has ignited an epidemic of epic proportion.

What's happening to our relaxation?

Relaxation or "R" is at an all-time low in our society. You know this! You can feel tension as soon as you enter a room. We have negative stress within our family, work, and friends. As a society there are more victims and judges than relaxed and confidant champions.

Worry is rampant. Anxiety is commonplace. Fear and panic is the residue. Negative stress is like water as it will find the path of least resistance and will soon flood all that it finds. Stress will stop a peak performer in their tracks. It hobbles the strong and cripples the weak. America needs relaxation and relaxation techniques, and she needs it now. Of course, it starts in the mirror as you peruse your inner dialogue and your outer being.

If your Relaxation Level is low, focus on it. This component of S.C.O.R.E.* is a major challenge with the overwhelming flood of negative information that bombards us daily. It's difficult to escape the grasp of the most competitive sports, academic, business and social environment in history. Stress has permeated society, from young children to the elderly and everyone in between. Life-work balance is out of whack!

Immunize yourself from all that stresses you. Be aware of your Relaxation Level at all times. Low "R" can permeate the other components of S.C.O.R.E.* and when this occurs your basic performances will suffer greatly.

The definition is:

Relaxation or R is being comfortable (free from anxiety, worry, and fear) while executing well-defined tasks that lead to well-defined goals and ultimately your Visions.

With the S.C.O.R.E.® System you'll soon reduce your breathing from approximately fifteen to seventeen breaths per minute to the Zone state of six to eight breaths per minute. Relaxation is just a few techniques away.

High R has jurisdiction over calmness, comfort, elegance, tranquility, peacefulness, stillness, composure, quietude, poise, smooth, effortlessness, grace, ease, and serenity.

Low R has jurisdiction over anxiety, worry, tense, frazzled, apprehension, concern, agitation, burden, fidgety, fear, dread, stressful, edgy, distress, panic, jumpy, jittery, nervousness, frightfulness, foreboding, alarm, trepidation, anger, and most other negative reactions to stress.

Rate your Relaxation and the Relaxation of each of your Arena Key People.

Enjoyment

He was world class. World champion was his quest. After a long workout of grueling self-punishment, I watched my client double over and begin to throw-up. He literally pushed himself to illness. While physically vomiting, he had a sinister, wicked smile on his face. I couldn't believe what I was seeing. As I approached to see if I could help him, he blurted out loudly, "I can't wait to make those bastards pay for how bad I feel!" I was stunned at this declaration from a man that was simultaneously laughing and vomiting. He was actually enjoying pushing himself to the brink of total exhaustion. At that moment I knew he would win. And he did.

It was a small venue of only sixty people. Cramped but cozy, the stage was poised for greatness. Slowly, the band walked on the stage. Behind the drums was the iconic **Mick Fleetwood** of the famous rock group **Fleetwood Mac**. Here at his club in Maui, Mick brought together the finest musicians for a public jam session. His face revealed his enjoyment from delivering his singular craft of providing the overall beat of the night. He said after the event, "I love to play. I love a 'live' crowd more than anything."

Champions love what they do and do what they love.

Enjoyment or "E" is literally and figuratively at the end of the word S.C.O.R.E.® and it's the end product of the S.C.O.R.E.® Success System itself.

The definition is:

Enjoyment or E is the passion, pleasure, and satisfaction while executing well-defined tasks that lead to well-defined goals and ultimately your Visions.

Most champions have brought passion to the forefront as they prepare, adjust, and evaluate their performances. The champion does NOT use the word "problem." This word is heavy, cumbersome, unwieldy, and negative in nature. We all hate problems! Interchange "problem" with the word "challenge" and that will motivate, inspire, and encourage you to find the solutions needed. Enjoyment will arrive.

You can have Enjoyment in your work arena and low Enjoyment once you arrive home and vice versa. Enjoyment is highly contagious. This aspect of S.C.O.R.E.® can elevate the performance of a team, company, or family.

High E has jurisdiction over thoughts that convey movement, desire, pleasure, rapture, hunger, eagerness, inspiration, motivation, stimulus, delight, elation, liveliness, stimulation, animation, thrill, encouragement, exhilaration, passion, craving, happiness, alertness, nimbleness, gladness, cheerfulness, contentment, glee, bliss, joyfulness, and ecstasy.

Low E has jurisdiction over sorrow, blues, melancholy, sadness, wretchedness, displeasure, anger, apathy, dispiritedness, laziness, lethargy, droopiness, boredom, lumbering, limpness, listlessness, discontentment, unconcern, indifference, unresponsiveness, unimportance, dullness, dreariness, lifelessness, flatness, insipidness, monotony, and unhappiness, among other maladies.

Rate your Enjoyment and the Enjoyment of each of your Arena Key People.

Which S.C.O.R.E.® marker needs your immediate attention?

▸ **S**elf-discipline
▸ **C**oncentration
▸ **O**ptimism
▸ **R**elaxation
▸ **E**njoyment

Rate Your Current Overall S.C.O.R.E.® Level:
(I to 10 with 10 high)

S.	C.	O.	R.	E.
__	__	__	__	__

Your Life Blueprint

Rate Your S.C.O.R.E.® Level

Rate your S.C.O.R.E.® Level for each Life Arena from 1 to 10, with 10 being the highest. Base the rating on reaching your Vision with its due date within each Life Arena. See the following example.

The person rated in the following table has a serious, low Relaxation Level especially within the Self, Finance, Work, and Son Arenas. The overall Finance Arena definitely needs more attention. The Sibling Arena needs work on Optimism. There is a lack of belief that the Vision will be accomplished.

Furthermore, the Work Arena is dangerously low with Relaxation and Enjoyment. You will soon have a Toolbox to choose pertinent

90-Second Rule™ tools and techniques to bolster your S.C.O.R.E.® Level and attract the Zone in all Life Arenas. Now The Blueprint will come alive and the building of your authentic, genuine best self will come to fruition.

Life Arenas	S	C	O	R	E	Total
Self	7	7	8	6	8	36
Son	8	8	8	6	6	36
Finance	6	5	8	5	5	29
Parent	7	8	8	6	8	37
Spouse	9	8	9	7	7	40
Brother	6	6	4	7	7	30
Work	8	6	7	6	6	33
Hobby	8	8	9	8	9	42
Home	8	5	8	8	8	37
Total	67	61	69	59	64	

Your Life Blueprint

Rate Your S.C.O.R.E.® Level

Rate your S.C.O.R.E.® Level for each Life Arena from 1 to 10, with 10 being the highest. Base the rating on reaching your Vision with its due date within each Life Arena.

Life Arenas	S	C	O	R	E	Total
Self						
Personal Finance						
Total						

CHAPTER 16

The 90-Second Rule™

Creating The Blueprint is step one. Step two is staying on course with the S.C.O.R.E.® System. The **90-Second Rule**™ is key among the collective tools, techniques, and tips that can keep your S.C.O.R.E.® Level simple and balanced.

As Americans we like things short, quick, and right NOW. Most decisions in your life can be decisively made within 90 seconds. The **90-Second Rule**™ was designed to do just that. Inside the S.C.O.R.E.® Success System is a collection of proven, concrete tips, tools, and techniques that can help improve the quality of your life, business, and sport without inconvenience. Period.

Why 90 seconds?

Since the age of fourteen years old, the 90-second time period has been very prevalent in my life. What you can accomplish within this time frame still amazes me.

90 seconds to increase sales.

The significance of ninety seconds became evident when I sold Fuller Brush products door-to-door as a teenager. Corporate statistics showed a good salesperson would sell one out of every three homes. Since most of the sales force was more than forty years old, I knew speed was not in their favor. "If I see more homes, I'll make more money," I thought. Soon I was sprinting between homes. More importantly, I knew within the first ninety seconds if I was going to make a sale or not. In fact, the 90-second routine of providing a small gift (basting brush, jar opener, hand lotion sample, and so on) in exchange for the occupant giving us ninety seconds to hear our pitch, worked like a charm. With eight young friends under my guidance, we led Kentucky in sales for the year, and I made more money than my mother and father combined.

90 seconds to change losing ways.

When the score in tennis is an odd total of games played such as 4-1, 3-2 or 5-2, the players change sides to prevent either player from having an advantage due to the wind or sun. This changeover period is ninety seconds. It was this short break where I could collect my thoughts and create a new tactic or recover physically. In my competitive tennis days, this 90-second period was crucial for reversing a poor performance into a winning way. "Attack his backhand," I thought. And if I didn't use this time judiciously, I lost. "I am so tired, I need to end the points quicker," I unwisely thought myself into losing ways.

In the mid-1970s, I began coaching the best tennis professionals in the world. Traveling full-time on the men's and women's pro circuits, I swiftly learned that the coach of the #1 player in the world was providing hand signals from the stands, which was against the rules. After one of my top fifty ranked players lost a match to the #1 player, it was evident that his coach changed the course of the match with his illegal signals. "This is unfair!" I vehemently complained to the governing body of men's professional tennis, the Association of Tennis Players (ATP.) "This guy is cheating, he's ripping us off," I continued to complain. I was told, "There's nothing we can do. We can't prove this." In this short meeting with the governing tennis body, they ended the conversation with, "Do what you need to do." With a wry smile, I realized they just gave me the green light to signal my own players. "Okay, I get it!"

During every ninety-second changeover, my sophisticated signals would soon be received and matches that were on the brink of defeat would swiftly turn into victory. Victories mounted and losses were reversed. The "no coaching" rule still applies in today's game (except in Davis Cup matches and qualifying rounds of the 2017 U.S. Open) but I'm certain it exists.

It takes less than ninety seconds to reverse losing ways and find victory. Today I train top amateur and professional tennis players to use simple, proven **90-Second Rule™** tools to attract the Zone and get his or her game back on track to winning ways. No (still illegal) outside coaching necessary. Ninety seconds is all it takes to influence friends, colleagues, clients, and even strangers.

90 seconds to see what you want.

A 90-second visualization will become your best friend. This packet of power has assisted all my clients' preparation for decades. In less than ninety seconds you can adjust and adapt all performances. And

90-second evaluations, without emotion, will cut to the chase on what you did right and what needs your immediate attention.

90-second visualization rocks! You can prepare, adjust, and evaluate like a champion in this short amount of time.

Be decisive.

Most life, business, and sports decisions can be made in less than 90 seconds. Make the most of your time. Use the next chapter's tools and techniques to erase chaos, fear, confusion, doubt, stress, anxiety, sadness, and every other mental malady known to man. Sprinkled judiciously throughout your day these tools will help you engage more in the moment, rather than spend the majority of your time in the past or future. It's time to maximize your quality of life. Period.

It takes less than 90 seconds to change your mind and reverse your course of action.

CHAPTER 17

The Universal 13™

There are thirteen 90-Second Rule™ tools that have been, will be, and are used by all of my clients. They are concrete, proven, and portable. They will work for all of your Life Arenas.

Keeping your S.C.O.R.E.® Level simple and balanced is the quest. These tools provide the mental capacity for turning The Blueprint into a living and breathing document of success.

Of the following thirteen tools, choose the ones that work best for you. Wield these tools judiciously before, during, and at the conclusion of each performance or day. They are transportable so take them with you to your work, golf course, tennis court, or other Life Arenas.

The S.C.O.R.E.® Check √

How many times have you performed in sports, business, relationships, or academics and wish you could have reversed the performance? How many times, if you had known about your negative body language, would the performance outcome have been different? How many times did trying too hard cost you strokes in your golf game? How many times did lack of Enjoyment at the beginning of the day cause a "Bad Day"?

To ensure that your performance is on track, you have to check your S.C.O.R.E.®—the five intangible mental markers that can collectively unlock your full potential. Everyone, regardless of age, can manage these performance indicators at any given time and place. Each person is responsible for calibrating them until they are balanced at their highest state. It is here that the peak performance of the Zone arrives, where everything is possible.

It is the self-awareness of S.C.O.R.E.® (Self-discipline, Concentration, Optimism, Relaxation, and Enjoyment) that provides the major key to being successful. Collectively these mental markers form a domino-like chain that governs your overall attitude.

What if you could be aware that your confidence was low before your clients, bosses, parents, teachers, or friends knew it? What if you could realize you are not relaxed and immediately do something about it? What if your friends and family never had to ask, "What's wrong?" That's because you already fixed the challenge before anyone knew it existed.

This would give you an advantage, right?

The S.C.O.R.E.® Check √ was designed to give you this advantage.

The S.C.O.R.E.® Check √ has been used since 1974. It has been wielded at Wimbledon, the Masters, Super Bowl, World Series, NBA Playoffs, and in corporate boardrooms of the Fortune 500. With practice, you will be able to brandish this tool for peak performance at any time.

Champions from all walks of life, not just superstar athletes, are using the S.C.O.R.E.® Check √ at periodic times throughout their day:

▶ The first thing in the morning
▶ Before, during, and after every performance
▶ At the conclusion of each day

The S.C.O.R.E.® Check √ is an integral part of the S.C.O.R.E.® Success System. It is a tool to assist you to balance your overall S.C.O.R.E.® Level, which is the key to a Zone performance. The Check √ is a way to ascertain your overall performance mood and it will identify your weakest links as you prepare, adjust, or evaluate your overall day or individual performances. It should take a maximum of ninety seconds.

Your S.C.O.R.E.® awareness will correct 90 percent of all performance challenges.

When using the S.C.O.R.E.® Check √, use or adjust the following questions to fit your Arena as well as your situation, condition, and circumstance. Here's how to use it. First, turn all of your attention to your thoughts, feelings, and sensations. Begin in order of the word S.C.O.R.E. Obviously, S is first, followed by C.O.R.E.

Self-discipline

- ▶ Do I have well-defined goals with strategies? (Yes or No)
- ▶ Do I have a well-defined schedule? (Yes or No)

If you become aware that your goals are cloudy or nonexistent, then get disciplined and organized. Review your goals for the performance or day ASAP.

Concentration

- ▶ Am I here in the now? (Yes or No)
- ▶ Am I ready to send focused energy to people and my goals? (Yes or No)

If you become aware that your concentration is lacking, then narrow your focus. Get in the NOW ASAP.

Optimism

- ▶ Do I believe? (Yes or No)
- ▶ Do I expect positive results? (Yes or No)

If you become aware that your optimism and/or confidence are low, then turn up your belief and expectancy. Raise your head high. Review your belief in the goals, strategy, and tactics for the day ASAP.

Relaxation

- ▶ Am I comfortable with my day (performance) and its goals and strategy? (Yes or No)
- ▶ Am I breathing six to eight breaths per minute? (Yes or No)

If you become aware that you are tense, worried, anxious, or uncomfortable, then get relaxed. Lower your breathing, release your jaw tension, and let go of the feelings of trying too hard.

Enjoyment

- ▶ Am I enjoying the process? (Yes or No)
- ▶ Am I ready to smile and be happy with passion? (Yes or No)

If you become aware that you are not having fun, get enthused the best you can. Pick up the pace, put on a smile, laugh out loud, sing or dance, and get ready for AWESOME.

The Morning S.C.O.R.E.® Check √ will kick-start an awesome day.

Remember: Balancing your S.C.O.R.E.® Level will attract the phenomenon called the Zone. Being aware of each performance and its intangibles will assist you in consistently managing this powerful mindset.

Sometimes just thinking the word S.C.O.R.E.® can do the job.

Tens of thousands of Zoniacs™ around the world are happy every day. Why not you? It takes less than ninety seconds. Start and finish your day in the Zone!

The Re-Boot Tool™

How do champions think less than the average person? How do they manage their thoughts? How do they right a sinking ship? How do they hold their focus for long periods of time? How do they manage the Zone?

If you could see a printout of an average person's thoughts you would quickly understand that they change subject matter hundreds of times daily, approximately every ten to fourteen seconds. Like a pinball in a pinball machine, their thoughts careen from the past to the future and back again in seconds. They easily bounce from negatives to positives and vice versa in a short period of time. As self-professed, great multitaskers, many people take great pride in attempting to manage mass quantities of info on a daily basis. Some info is golden and beneficial while some is useless and even detrimental. Approximately sixty percent of the average person's waking hours is spent in natural chaos. They think too much.

Champions DO NOT think like everyone else.

What do champions do when they begin to feel flummoxed, confused, or bewildered? What do they do when their mind wanders during an important event? What do they think to prevent worry? What do they do when they realize they're performing in the Zone? What do they think when they feel the Zone slipping away?

The answer for thousands of champions around the world is the highly effective **Re-Boot Tool**™ and it's the most often used of the hundreds of 90-Second Rule™ tools. Someone on this planet has wielded it every day for over forty years. It has been deployed on the mound during the World Series. It's helped write *New York Times* best selling novels. This tool has been used on hundreds of golf courses around the world, most notably at the Masters° in Augusta. Ten golfers used it to win their first professional tournament. Athletes, sales personnel, students, parents, managers, and entrepreneurs are more than likely using this tool right now.

Your brain is like a computer. When your computer has too many programs open and you've been switching rapidly between them, your hard drive can slow down, lock up or freeze. Your brain can do the same. What do you do? Use the **Re-Boot Tool**™.

The **Re-Boot Tool**™ takes ten to ninety seconds depending on the situation, circumstance, or condition. It's used to initially attract, regain, or maintain the peak performance mindset of the Zone.

Here's the 7-step **Re-Boot Tool**™ technique:

1. Shut your eyes (optional and preferable).
2. Unhinge your jaw.
3. Take several deep breaths with long exhales.
4. With eyes closed, place a blank or dark screen in your mind's eye and hold this image for ten to ninety seconds. During this brief time, you will have no thoughts of the past or future. None. Clear all thoughts away from your mind.
5. After your mind is clear, raise your head up high.
6. Open your eyes.
7. Refocus on the task at hand and send your mental energy outward to specific targets, objectives, or goals.

When you make a costly mistake or error, Re-Boot. When you are overthinking the situation or circumstance, Re-Boot. When you are freaked out about what may happen next, Re-Boot. When you feel yourself getting frustrated, impatient, embarrassed, or upset, Re-Boot. When you are tired, Re-Boot. When you receive bad news, Re-Boot. When you feel your chest tighten from stress, Re-Boot. When you start to care too much about what other people think, Re-Boot. If the victim in you surfaces, Re-Boot. When you begin to judge others, Re-Boot.

You will also want to Re-Boot when things are going well. When you are aware of being in the Zone, you've just left this awesome mindset. Re-Boot to get it back. If you are totally locked in the Zone, Re-Boot to elongate the Zone's "purposeful calm" feeling. To ensure stretching the Zone phenomenon, prepare to use it prior to the performance.

In 2002, former MLB All-Star **Mike Cameron** became the first and only player to hit four home runs in five innings. He became the sixteenth player in history to hit four home runs in one game. Before the game, Mike wasn't feeling well. "Jimmy, I can't see the ball very well. I'm not comfortable at the plate," Mike told me with weakness in his voice. "Every time you feel uncomfortable or have a negative thought, Re-Boot," I encouraged. After two home runs in the first inning, he Re-Booted in order to elongate the Zone. After his third home run, he Re-Booted multiple times prior to his fourth at-bat. "I hit solid," was Mike's only thought. After his fourth home run, he Re-Booted again. During his fifth at-bat, he was hit with a pitch and the home crowd even booed their own pitcher. Mike Re-Booted. "I'm in the now," he affirmed.

In Mike Cameron's sixth and final at-bat, he smashed a drive deep to the warning track to end his historical night. All of Mike's Re-Boots enabled him to stay in the Zone and be the best he could be. "Tonight was surreal. The Zone was like a dream," reflected a confident Cameron.

To attract, prolong, and stay in the Zone, champion golfers often Re-Boot six to twelve times during a round. A champion tennis player Re-Boots during ninety second changeovers. A sales champion Re-Boots before every sales presentation. An "A" student Re-Boots while taking an important exam. A successful platform speaker Re-Boots before he or she walks on the stage.

Re-Boot before physically and mentally changing Life Arenas. Re-Boot before you enter your workplace. Re-Boot before you go home. Clear your mind of the clutter. Free yourself from overanalyzing. Turn off your brain and give it a deserved rest. Re-Boot at least four times daily.

The **Re-Boot Tool**™ is universal in keeping you on track. It is portable, easily deployed, and used by people from all walks of life in every age group. If Concentration is what you want, then place The **Re-Boot Tool**™ in your mental toolbox.

Be in the Zone. Use the **Re-Boot Tool**™ to be the best you can be.

The Light Switch™

Like a light switch, your head can be raised in an up or down position. Try this simple exercise:

Place a negative image or picture in your mind's eye. Sorry to have you do this, but the point of the exercise will be revealed within seconds. This specific negative thought will stay with you the entire exercise. Now raise your chin above parallel and after a few seconds lower your chin to your chest...raise your head again in an upright position and lower it one last time.

Approximately seventy-five percent of all audience members throughout the years reported the following: When their heads were raised, the negative image either disappeared or they had to conjure it back into their minds. When their heads were in a down position the negative thought was clear, robust and concise in their mind. Try it. See for yourself.

If you experienced what the vast majority of my audience members experienced, then the Light Switch™ tool is for you. Raise your head up when negatives appear or a negative just occurred. A MLB pitcher uses the Light Switch™ just after he throws a pitch that is hit for a home run out of the ballpark. A PGA or LPGA golfer raises his or her head after they hit a tee shot into the rough.

By raising your head to adversity, you negate the chance of replaying the act or deed in a negative way. You will also use this universal tool to find solutions to challenges. Have a challenge? Raise your head and look up to your right and the solution will more readily be forthcoming.

Breathe Like a Baby™

Do you ever get the butterflies before a meeting, important conference call, or public speaking performance? The butterflies occur when blood vessels and capillaries in your stomach constrict so your blood is diverted to the brain for clarity and to the large muscles so you have inordinate strength, quickness, speed, and agility. Your body is just ready to go into its Zone state.

This is how you can relax when the pressure is the greatest. This tool takes less than ninety seconds to apply. Here's what to do:

1. Unhinge your jaw and relax your face and neck
2. Place either hand over your stomach near your belly button
3. With each inhale, draw your belly button closer to your spine or backbone.
4. With each exhale, move your belly button away from your spine or backbone
5. After six to eight breaths, you will feel your shoulders relax and tension will begin to leave your body.

Sometimes you need to Breathe Like a Baby.™

This technique is how infants fall asleep so easily. It's also how your dog can be fetching a ball...then you get on your cell...and when you finally look for your dog, she or he is sleeping and maybe even snoring. Both the baby and dog relax by using this 90-Second Rule™ technique.

That's right! It takes less than ninety seconds for this tool to take effect. You will feel more relaxed. Now send all of your energy away from you to a well-defined target or objective. You're ready to launch a positive energy flow. Use this technique anytime and anywhere.

Remember: your supposed "nervousness" was just your body preparing to "Be in the Zone." Now you know what to do.

The Palm Tree Tool™

The palm tree reacts to a hurricane or violent storm by allowing the force of the wind to pass through it. Bending but not breaking, it absorbs the wrath of the devastating storm. After the hurricane dissipates and disappears, the palm stands up straight to see another day of sunshine. It symbolizes all that's good about the sun, the beach, the ocean, recreation, and pleasure. Adjusting to its environment helps it survive and thrive.

Have the image of the palm tree ready to be uploaded into your mind at all times. Arm yourself with this "peaceful and pleasant" picture anytime a human hurricane comes your way. Within the first 90 seconds of a verbal or nonverbal assault, relax your jaw and reduce your breathing. Say nothing. No knee-jerk reaction of anger or counterattack. Allow the negativity to pass through you just the awesome palm.

So the next time you are confronted by an angry driver on the road, a disgruntled loved one who is blowing off steam, or a negative text that could easily disrupt your Zone demeanor, be the palm tree!

An oak tree, of course, would brace itself and immediately fight the 80 to 100 mph forces. These two opposing forces usually end up with the oak tree's branches broken and the possibility of being completely uprooted. Many of us react to the life hurricanes of negativity in the same way. We become overly aggressive when faced with confrontation. We do not bend. In fact, we might even counter-attack the attacker. We close our minds to a peaceful resolution. We stay tethered to the drama. It is these reactions that prolong disputes and even add fuel to the negative forces that found you.

Are you a palm tree or an oak tree in the face of adversity? Most of the time a palm tree attitude works and the demeanor of an oak tree seldom works. Although if the situation presents itself, you may need to stand tall like the mighty oak and say, "This is not acceptable."

Keep both the palm tree and oak tree images in your mind. Be armed when the time comes to apply their services. Be aware of your thoughts and feelings and you will control your actions and ultimately your results.

Cheetah Focus™

The cheetah quietly crawled in the tall grass in anticipation of dinner. It looked like it hadn't eaten for days. Slowly, it edged its way to the clearing where a herd of impala nervously grazed. Ever so stealthily, the lean predator eyed his prey. From the large group of mild-mannered animals, a singular victim was selected. The energy from the cheetah pierced the grass. You could feel it. Like a laser, it locked on the exposed jugular of his singular dinner-to-be. With the swiftness of a blur, the cat sprang into the clearing. The terrified herd scattered in panic.

Then an amazing thing occurred. A pregnant impala fell in the path of the charging cheetah. Instead of stopping for an easy victory, the cat leapt over the fallen mother-to-be and continued the pursuit of his original selection. More than a half dozen impala were passed up. The focus was on the biggest of the herd...the largest prize. Soon, with speed and tenacity the hunt was over. The original prey was caught.

Witnessing this frightening scene, I was stunned by what is natural in a world where only the strong survive. This was focus. This was single-mindedness. This was the epitome of not going where the grass is greener. The cheetah could easily have changed his intended prey in the middle of the hunt. No. The predator's mind was set. One purpose. One focus. This was the ultimate form of concentration.

Luckily, we do not have to personally hunt for our food. But we do hunt for sales. We hunt for grades. We hunt for better relationships. We hunt for opportunity. We hunt for the keys to manage other people. We hunt to attain personal records and good fortune. We are hunters. And a better quality of life is our ultimate prey.

But are we focused? Do we send our physical and mental energies to small well-defined destinations?

Are we focused on opportunity? How can we see opportunity if we're not prepared? Sometimes it knocks very softly. If we're worried about the past, we'll miss it. If we're anxious for the future, we'll never know opportunity was near. We must be ready. We must focus.

Does the cheetah think, "Maybe the impala is too fast." No. "What if I get hurt?" No. "Oh, which one will I catch?" No. The cheetah has little thought. He's focused.

Many of us are scattered. We chase the whole herd and catch nothing. We throw a multitude of ideas on the wall and hope one will stick. That's not the cheetah. He would go hungry with this mindset. Select what you want. Then go for it. Put on your blinders. Jump over the other impala. Focus. Period!

The successful performer's mantra is: "I have no future. I have no past. My goal is to make the present last." The hunter that stays in the present sees opportunity. He knows how to seize it. He is focused. No coulda', shoulda', woulda', gotta', gonna' in his vocabulary. "I am!" This is a great hunter's thought.

Concentration is being in the Now. You can only concentrate when you send your energy away from you to specific targets. Laser-like.

When selling, focus on the buyer. He's telling you if he's uncomfortable with your pitch. He's telling you if he's not confident with your service or product. He's telling you his needs. Focus on them. He's telling you he's buying. So quit selling and close! Focus like the cheetah. Listen. Look. Get in the Now!

When playing tennis, focus on the ball as it leaves your opponent's racket. Focus on your foe scrambling for your deep corner drive. See the weak return and pounce on it out of the air for an easy volley into the open court. Champions make their opponent feel their focus. Baseball hitters focus on the pitcher's release point. "I hit solid!" is their baseball mantra. In golf, you'll never see the sand trap or water hazard unless you take your eye off of the flag. Send your energy down the fairway to your target.

Focus. You've set your goals. Attack one at a time. Now send them your energy. Be the cheetah!

Magic Mantra™

This is the "I Am" tool. "I'm awesome." "I'm accurate." "I'm relaxed." I'm healthy." These are all positive affirmations that can bolster confidence, maximize concentration, enhance relaxation, and facilitate super healing. Why do they work so effectively? Your subconscious mind does NOT know the difference between fantasy and reality.

Direct your affirmation to the challenge at hand. Say and/or think it to yourself. Place the image you want on your mental screen. This tool is simple, portable, and it applies to anything you do.

QuickChange™

Sometimes the quickest change in a performance is to switch from passive to aggressive or vice versa. Picking up the pace has accelerated Zone arrival. A salesperson is having a non-sales day and picking up the rhythm can jumpstart more connectivity with prospects. Slowing down the tempo with a corresponding demeanor can alter a vacation that's off on the wrong foot with all in the family bickering, indecisive, and not on the same page. A baseball pitcher slows down the pace between pitches and the hitter is thrown off-balance by his impatience with a slower tempo.

Behavior change is swift and easy. Changing how you sit in your classroom or conference room can be an instant S.C.O.R.E.® Maker. Stand up tall before entering a room and this behavior change will attract more positive attention as you arrive.

Restructure Now

Changing strategy and tactics can swiftly alter the performance. It can confuse, demoralize, and de-energize the competition, as well as lift you to a Zone performance. My clients have altered their performances with strategic and tactical changes countless times.

The key to approaching a goal in a different way is to be armed with multiple options. These strategies and tactics require practice before unleashing them in "real time."

Show Some Teeth (Sometimes Skip)

Smile. We now know that every person has "mirror neurons" in their body that reflect what they see when they meet someone. A smile from you will automatically produce a smile in someone else. How powerful is that? One smile and you can uplift another human being. This type of giving will make you feel amazing. This is simple, fast, and impactful.

Quick, toothy smiles while confronting a challenge can swiftly fuel-inject endorphins and dopamine into your bloodstream and you will feel the difference immediately. Smiles uplift you. Smiles keep your "E" Level elevated and this may be all you need to balance your S.C.O.R.E.° and attract the Zone.

Some of my clients even skip in order to produce the same effect. Former PGA star and current Champions Tour player **David Frost** skipped while playing a round during the Masters and former NFL center **Evan Pilgram** even skipped into the huddle of an NFL game. Sometimes you smile. Other times you might skip. Try both. You know you want to skip right now, don't you?

Music: Pipeline to the Zone

The Zone found me during a tennis match in Germany. I played awesomely and won. Why did the Zone show up? I was listening to music just before the match and I mentally carried the tune with me throughout my performance. This scenario has been shared with me by hundreds of performers.

It's the steady rhythm of the song's beats that inspires, motivates and encourages. Check out most television images of athletes in pre-game mode and most are wearing headphones. Like the soundtrack of a great movie, personal music can act as a soundtrack for your next performance. Yes...music can be a swift pipeline to the Zone.

Zone Hello & Goodbye

Calling all Zoniacs™! It's time we start making changes in the world. Right now! Commit to sharing positive energy with your friends, family, and strangers alike. We can do this!

Every day, people on the phone or in person ask me, "How are you?" My answers range from "Fannin-tastic!" to "Awesome!" to "Two levels above awesome!" The person asking is typically flummoxed by my response. The mood of the conversation is now fuel-injected with positive energy and the conversation tone is set.

Upgrade the first ninety seconds you see anyone. Also, do your part by upgrading the last ninety seconds when you say goodbye.

Get in the Zone. Transfer your Zone energy with every hello and goodbye. Most of us greet people the same way: "Hi," "How are you?" "What's up?" We take this greeting for granted. Many times our voice inflection and tonality are void of sincerity and feeling. Eye contact is typically missing. Our body language does not reflect the "I'm so glad to meet you or see you" mindset. Our goodbyes need to go to a higher level as well. It's time to toss out the old and bring in the new "Energy Creator Greeting and Salutation."

Champions bring a higher level of energy and optimism to the exchange of hello and good-bye. When someone greets you with "How are you?" reply with "Amazing!" or "Great!" or "Fantastic!" You choose the greeting. Make it simple. Mix it up. But by all means be consistent. When you say goodbye, leave the person or group with a positive, energetic farewell: "Godspeed." "Be Safe." "See you soon." "I look forward to seeing you again." "Stay in the Zone." This is simple.

Next...look them in the eye, long enough to discern eye color. Your gaze into their eyes should be about three to six seconds. Any longer than that and they may think you're weird. Don't overdo it! Full engagement in your greeting and salutation says, "I want to be in your presence right now." "I value you." "I want you to be happy." "I'll miss you." "Please...take some of my positive energy with you."

Finally, add the person's name multiple times to the greeting and goodbye. In fact, saying a stranger's name at least three times within the first ninety seconds of meeting will dramatically increase your ability of remembering their name. Personalizing your openings and closings goes a long way towards forging strong bonds. There's nothing better than personalizing positivity. Try it!

Make this newfound exchange with family, friends and strangers a part of every day. Be consistent. Mean what you say. And especially let the people you know feel the change.

I promise you will see the difference. People you meet and greet this way will be in awe. Your new hello and good-bye will blow people away. You will see and feel how your positive energy has an immediate impact.

When I get on an airplane, the flight attendant always asks, "How are you?" When I reply with my "I'm awesome!" or "I'm two levels higher than awesome!" response, some may think: "Get the Taser ready for seat 3C. He's acting strange. He's a little too positive."

Positively attack strangers with all of your mental and physical energy. Hose them down with a tsunami of positivity. Leave them in a wake of uplifting force that is soon passed on to the other people they meet.

Go out and make a difference in another person's day. It's time we change the world one person at a time.

Goodbye Zoniac™. Goodbye Champion. You can do this. Go deliver the goods!

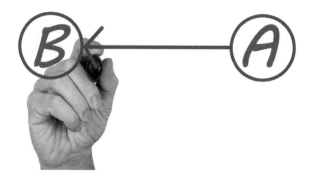

The B2A Principle™

For more than forty years, a top secret tool has been used by the best athletes and corporate leaders in the world. With this confidential success principle of managing their performances, records have been shattered and dreams have turned into reality. The B2A Principle™ is an integral part of the potent S.C.O.R.E.® Success System. Now let this simple application be revealed.

We've been taught at an early age that to reach any destination in life you must go from point A to point B. However, champions that I've personally coached have used a different approach that has proven successful.

Every vision and goal for all my clients has been reverse engineered chronologically from point B back to the starting point A. This tedoius process ultimately illuminates a pathway to walk on from A to B.

Let's say you want to lose twenty-five pounds in four months. When this arbitrary date is reached, you will weigh 200 pounds. By starting with the end result in mind and reversing what you will do the day before it occurs and then the week before and the month before, it ensures you will stay on track until the goal is complete.

With an imagined, illuminated pathway like a runway at an airport at night, your discipline will be locked in place. You will have concrete milestones that serve as mile markers for your weight-loss journey.

If you fall off the pathway for any reason, it's still illuminated for you to find your way back.

Use the B2A Principle™ for speeches, meetings, important phone calls, or any other performance that you desire. Just before I give a speech in front of thousands in the audience, I think, "What do I want these people to think once they are alone in their car driving home?" Try this before your next meeting. Ask yourself, "What do I want these people to think and ultimately do after this meeting is over?"

"Hmmm...what do I want you to think and do once you put down this book?" B2A.

TOP SECRET

CHAPTER 18

The "Crucial" Last 30 Minutes

It was 1:30 a.m. My client and I had evaluated his performance and he was finally preparing for sleep. With hot, fresh cookies and a glass of milk, he intently listened to my every word of guided imagery preparing him for the next game. As he mentally envisioned walking to the plate, I mentally was on the mound as the opposing pitcher. I said in a slow whisper as he lay in bed about to drift off into a deep R.E.M state, "Four seam fastball, middle in. On the rubber, wind-up, balance point, pitch!" As the word "pitch" pierced the air, my client envisioned the ball's release, remained stoic and calm, and finally stroked a home run off of one of the game's best pitchers. This situational imagery lasted no more than ten minutes. Finally he drifted asleep and I let myself out of his room and retired for the night. I knew what would take place in his mind as he slept through the night.

The guided imagery session described here has been carried out in some form or another for more than 2,500 clients worldwide. It's conducted by phone, Skype, and in person. Turning powerful mental images into reality by programming the subconscious is the quest.

This book is about creating The Blueprint and turning it into reality. You are on your way. This chapter, however, is crucial for manifesting The Blueprint into its physical equivalent.

There are two times in a twenty-four-hour cycle when your subconscious mind is naturally amenable to suggestion. They are right before you sleep and as you awake. Like fertile soil, your subconscious mind will readily receive good seeds and bad seeds during these times.

From the time you wake up to the time you go to sleep, every thought, feeling, and sensation is recorded by your subconscious mind and they are placed in a holding area in your mind for easy access. As you drift off to sleep, all of these thoughts and feelings are downloaded or replayed approximately *one to two times* during the night. The purpose of this replay is to store the information. If it's important, it will be filed for easier access. If it's not important, it's still stored but it may or may not have easy access.

Even more importantly, every thought, feeling and sensation during the last thirty minutes before you go to sleep is also recorded. However, these thoughts and feelings will be replayed *fifteen to seventeen times*.

YIKES! That's significant. And you wonder why you have nightmares, restless nights, and little sleep. Now you know.

This last thirty minutes before sleep period is obviously a big deal. The repetition of the replay is what programs the subconscious mind for success or failure. After seven to ten days in a row of thinking the same, basic thoughts (good or bad), stress is placed on the subconscious to manifest itself into its physical equivalent, **EVEN IF IT'S NOT GOOD FOR YOU**. Basically, whatever you think about during this time, you are likely to get.

This has been my secret tool for all my clients since 1974. I've literally sat in a chair in a hotel room like the scenario above guiding a client in Task, Situational, or Symbolic Visualization within thirty minutes of them sleeping.

This has worked for EVERY client in business, sports, and life.

Unfortunately for many people, they go to sleep thinking what they don't want. This replay can and probably does wreak havoc on the unsuspecting sleeper. They have no clue that they have sabotaged their success. They are the sole reason for failure, despair, anxiety, and even illness.

For example, a neighbor experienced the tragedy of her son's accidental death. For weeks, she went to sleep with the thought of her unfortunate loss. The nightly, multiple replay of her devastating loss pulled her into a deep depression. She began to lose substantial weight. The thoughts of wishing she was dead permeated her mind. She refused to leave her house. Her "I don't want to live anymore" thoughts accelerated. The anxiety became overwhelming as the replay of this tragic event occupied the majority of her thoughts. Within weeks of this type of thinking, she was diagnosed with breast cancer. Her wish was coming true. I relayed the above information and implored her to take heed of its crucial nature. Today, she has thankfully fully recovered.

Be careful what you think at night.

It is the life champion who goes to bed happy and gets up happy. They deal with what occurs between these opening and closing periods of a typical day.

Go to bed happy and get up happy.

The "Crucial" Last 30 Minutes should be utilized for visualizing what you want. Task, Situational, Symbolic and Aftermath visualization will elevate your performances once they're deployed at the end of your day. This is the game-changer you've been waiting to receive. Be consistent. Be positive.

Goodnight, Champion. Sleep well.

PART 3

Your Life Blueprint

**Your individual, stand-alone Life Arenas will be fully
discussed with "real" Visions, Big Rocks, and Tasks.**

CHAPTER 19

Your Self Arena

This Life Arena is showcased first because most of us focus on it last. This is all about me, myself, and I. Your Self Arena is critical for your overall well-being. It houses all of your values, principles, and morals. This Arena impacts your character.

How many bosses, parents, coaches, teachers, trainers, managers, and any other person who is influencing, guiding, and motivating their charges, work on what's best for him or her?

Do you work on improving you?

Your Self Arena impacts every other aspect of your life, business, or sport. It houses every general thought from your mental, physical, and spiritual perspective.

Your Self Arena blankets all daily thoughts pertaining to (just) you. If you brush your teeth, it is this activity that is under the umbrella of your Self Arena. When you think about your next meal or you want to get in shape, these thoughts reside under your Self Arena. So do your thoughts about your religion or spirituality.

Have you ever heard the following joke, "Well enough about me… let's talk about you? So…what do you think about me?" This chapter is all about YOU. Dedicate to building this part of The Blueprint for improving your inner and outer selves.

Use the following questions to determine, "What about me?"

1. Do I eat a minimum of three well-balanced meals daily?
2. Do I hydrate enough so that my urine is clear?
3. Do I get a minimum of seven hours of deep sleep each night?
4. Do I think and/or talk to myself with positive affirmations?
5. Do I avoid harmful overindulgences?
6. Do I choose friends that make me mentally, physically, and spiritually better?
7. Do I swiftly manage the stress in my life?
8. Do I only go into the past for non-emotional evaluation or to reminisce in a positive way with a friend?
9. Do I only go into the future for planning my Visions and Big Rocks with corresponding tactics and strategies?
10. Do I do what I love and love what I do?

11. Do I only think of what I want, as opposed to what I don't want in life?
12. Do I prioritize a daily, weekly, monthly, quarterly, and yearly Task list?
13. Do I take periodic breaks, mini-vacations, and full vacations to rejuvenate my mind, body, and soul?
14. Do I do for other people what I would want them to do for me?
15. Do I treat myself like a champion?
16. Am I my own best friend?

If the answer is "No" to any of these questions, then make it right. Create an action plan, if necessary. Commit to it. See yourself turning each "No" into a "Yes." See them in finished state. If the answer is "Yes," then congratulations, champion! You are on the right path.

Place this short questionnaire in safekeeping. Use it periodically to see if you're treating your best friend, YOU, like a champion. With the strains of the economy and the demands of society increasing, it is time to place your awareness on YOU.

Most of my clients that initially arrived at my doorstep put themselves last. They had placed their "happy eggs" in baskets of career, relationships or parenting, neglecting the very thing that makes everything possible.

How do you become your best friend?

Love yourself and it will be easier to showcase love for others and find reciprocating love. Respect yourself and you'll gain respect from others. Speak positively to yourself and positive people and opportunities will more readily arrive.

You know certain words and phrases received from others can negatively manipulate you. Once you turn these statements into your own words and phrases, your subconscious mind will become negative, and negative results will arrive. You know this.

Avoid self-deprecating humor and eliminate negative phrases that you direct to yourself.

- ▸ "I figured that would happen."
- ▸ "If I didn't have bad luck, I wouldn't have any luck at all."
- ▸ "I'm such an idiot!" or "I suck at..."
- ▸ "I'm too old for this."
- ▸ "I told you that wouldn't work."
- ▸ "That's just the way it goes."
- ▸ "I can't expect to succeed all of the time."
- ▸ "I win some and lose some."
- ▸ "There's not enough time in the day."
- ▸ "Why try? It's not appreciated. It does me no good."

Have you uttered any of the above phrases? No more put downs or beating yourself up, especially in front of others. No more self-deprecating fat jokes. No more victim and or judgmental thoughts or statements.

End negative self-talk.

If your daily, inner dialogue could be printed out, it would reveal if you are a best friend to yourself or not. I've told many clients,

"If I talked to you like you talk to you, you'd fire me."

Sell you on you. As your self-worth increases, a magnetic force of attraction will expand. This will bring to you most of the things you need and want in life. *Remember, you can take care of #1 without being arrogant, cocky, or boastful.*

It's time to "Be Your Own Best Friend."

Your Self Blueprint

The following Visions, Big Rocks, Tasks, and Key People have been acquired from The Blueprint of thousands of clients. Place strategic timelines for each of the following and incorporate them within your overall generic calendar. You are worth this time investment.

Possible Self Visions *(add, edit, or delete as you see fit)*: Be my genuine, authentic best self; be mentally, physically, and spiritually balanced; be my best mentally, physically, and spiritually; live a simple, balanced, and abundant life.

Possible Self Big Rocks *(add, edit, or delete as you see fit)*: Weigh 185 pounds; hire a nutritionist; attend church regularly; lose twenty pounds; join a health club; take yoga classes; eliminate swearing; stop smoking; drink alcohol in moderation; become extremely positive; use the S.C.O.R.E.® System; buy a new wardrobe; become a better listener; bolster optimism.

Possible Self Tasks *(add, edit, or delete as you see fit)*: Incorporate new response of "I'm awesome!" to all "How are you?" questions; wake up at 6:30 a.m. and go to sleep at 10:30 p.m. every night; drink 100 ounces of H_2O daily; use the Re-Boot Tool™ during golf rounds; research yoga instruction; practice positive self-talk for forty-eight hours; take inventory of my closet.

Possible Self Key People *(add, edit, or delete as you see fit)*: Personal trainer; yoga instructor; therapist; theologians; philosophers; mentors; coaches; teachers; minister or priest; dietician; spouse; massage therapist; hair stylist; life coach; psychiatrist; counselor; psychologist; doctor; parents; grandparents; godparents; uncles; aunts; dentist; best friend; fashion coordinator; and so on.

This group of people can dramatically influence your mindset and overall well-being. They can have influence over weight loss, drug and/or alcohol abuse, mental illness, time management, organizational skills, spirituality, and longevity.

Rate your Self S.C.O.R.E.® Level: (1 to 10 with 10 being high)

S.   C.   O.   R.   E.

___   ___   ___   ___   ___

CHAPTER 20

Your Relationship Arena

For ten years, this couple was the epitome of the "super couple." Their relationship was amazing. They were the envy of their friends. Human interactions like this are filled with love, trust, affection, and friendship. These unions are the gold standard for couples. But something changed.

There were no indiscretions. No major fights. They just grew apart. Then one day the wife was visibly depressed. Her business suffered. Her husband came home later and later. The kids noticed and asked, "What's wrong?" Each of their parents noticed the change of hearts and tried to intervene, but to no avail. What happened? How and why did everything else come apart?

With every positive, healthy, and vibrant relationship, there are others that have negative and even abusive connections. How does a strong relationship crumble?

The Relationship Arena is by far the toughest Arena.

When two people decide to live together, their relationship changes, hopefully for the better. At the beginning, both parties are fully engaged and committed to their positive union. But with time, this Arena winds up with two simultaneous coaches, unlike other Life Arenas. This has the potential for both harmony and discord. I've never seen two coaches guiding a winning team at the same time.

What happens to good marital intentions? Added to your union are new challenges from your Personal Finance, Parenting, Job, and Self Arenas. Inequality in paychecks, conflicting work hours, the financial demands of a house and raising children, disagreements on parenting philosophy and principles, and the demands of two careers can prey on one's sanity. When you factor in lack of sleep, little or no exercise, mental and physical fatigue, it's easy to allow the scale to tip toward conflict. This dynamic can readily spawn thoughts of change that seem unlikely to occur. Frustration, negativity, anguish, hopelessness, and despair can all enter the mindset or mindsets of a well-intended marital partnership.

A marriage is not 50/50 percent in managing this intimate, emotional portion of your life. Here are a few examples. It can be 80/20 percent in managing household finances or even 100/0 percent. It can be 90/10 percent in managing your home, 60/40 percent in intimacy, and 30/70 percent in daily parenting. These numbers can change and even be reversed depending on the condition, situation, and circumstance.

Couples who compromise remain couples.

Unlike other Arenas, this Arena is tough because it is intimate and packs every possible emotion. But it's worth it. The mental, physical, emotional, and spiritual bonds that can be formed with two people make this Arena one of wonderment and awe. Couples are blessed to find this and it is available to all who enter this sacred union.

When you first met her (or him), the atmosphere was electric. "I love being with her" is your thought and feeling. After departing, her image became indelibly emblazoned in your mind. Instantly, you could conjure up the scent of her perfume or his cologne. This made you smile. Quickly, the image of his or her smile, tilt of their head, rhythm of their gait, and other unique mannerisms permeated your brain. These mental pictures consumed you. He or she popped into your mind during business meetings, a round of golf and other obscure times.

Simultaneously, "your significant other" was picturing you. You thought of living together in a beautiful home on the ocean. She thought of you playing golf with your son. Shared vision slowly but surely began to take hold of both minds. Finally, you asked for her hand in marriage and she willingly accepted. A shared vision of a future life together was being transformed from a vision to reality.

Shared vision brought you together
and the absence of it will tear you apart.

Here's the flipside to this fairytale love affair.

Do I want you to divorce? Absolutely NOT! Once you understand how the seeds of divorce are created and can innocently spread throughout your relationship, you will be more aware on what to avoid.

Because the last thirty minutes before bedtime is so significant, the person you sleep with during that period is the most important person in your life. Period! The seeds of divorce are sprinkled throughout the relationship long before the culmination of parting and it's based on the thoughts occurring during this time. Here's what happens.

You or your significant other begin to have thoughts about another person or may look at another person in a romantic or sexual way. Possibly, both of you begin quarreling and one or both begin to think negative thoughts of the other. "She's such a jerk!" he thinks. "I hate how he acts!" she mutters to herself. "He or she is such an *#$%@*!" is thought with disgust after reality doesn't match their expectation.

These thoughts slowly spawn negative actions and non-actions. Negativity can finally find its way into the bedroom during the last thirty minutes before you sleep. Resentment, jealousy, guilt, and animosity can dash the flames of passion, creating a dynamic of being a victim and a judge as well as physical isolation. Even though this can occur slowly, it can spread rapidly, clouding reason with emotion. Be careful what you think. And if you do think negatively, it will take an inordinate amount of positive thoughts to overcome the negative ones.

Positive thoughts are what brought you together in the first place. Remember? Before you got married, you thought about that person a lot. Eventually, you and that person thought the same thing, and many times it occurred simultaneously when you were apart. That is why you blew up their phone throughout the day and night. Shared vision was the seed to growing the relationship into a dynamic union of everlasting love and devotion.

Your relationship is only as strong as what you think when your partner is not there.

When you're apart and you have no thoughts about your significant other or you're only thinking of someone else, these thoughts are recorded and replayed multiple times during your sleep. If you have negative thoughts about your "significant other" being a nag, mean, nonresponsive, or indifferent regarding sex, affection, or romance, those thoughts before sleep will program your subconscious to turn it into its physical equivalent. It will happen!

Many couples have stopped going to bed at the same time. You should. During **The "Crucial" Last 30 Minutes** (Chapter 18) before sleep, take time to just touch, kiss, or say sweet nothings. *Absolutely* avoid talk about children, finance, or jobs. If there is any talk at all, make it only about shared vision of your collective future. Otherwise, it's just a time to be with each other in an intimate way.

Going to bed in a very positive mindset with your significant other is crucial.

Apply this to waking up as well. First thing in the morning, think of your significant other. If he or she has left the bed earlier, get up and find your significant other. Give yourself up to ninety seconds to just say, "Good morning! How are you? I hope you have a great day!" And if you leave the house before he or she wakes, leave them a note saying, "Have an awesome day. I love you!" This will frame your day with a positive attitude towards your relationship and it will do the same for your best friend.

The bottom line is we can think ourselves into a divorce just as easily as we can think ourselves into a great, loving, nurturing relationship. Think about what you think about. Take nothing for granted. And don't forget the last thirty minutes before you go to sleep.

Your Relationship Blueprint

The following Visions, Big Rocks, Tasks, and Key People have been acquired from The Blueprint of thousands of clients. Place strategic timelines for each of the following and incorporate them within your overall generic calendar. Your "significant other" is worth the time investment.

Possible Relationship Visions *(add, edit, or delete as you see fit)***:**
- 1+1=3 (You and I together equal more than apart)
- Mentally, physically, and spiritually connected
- Soul mates
- Unconditional life partners
- Mental, physical, and spiritual best friend

Possible Relationship Big Rocks *(add, edit, or delete as you see fit)***:**
- Adhere to the 90-Second Rule™
- Weekly date night
- Vacation (without children)
- Eat dinner together nightly
- Listen proactively
- Avoid sarcasm and verbal put-downs
- Build positive self-esteem
- Help partner relax
- Add spontaneity
- Add the element of surprise
- Go to bed happy
- Wake up happy
- Respect partner's dreams and desires
- Be more intimate
- Go to bed together
- Avoid arguing in front of the children
- Support partner's career

Possible Relationship Tasks *(add, edit, or delete as you see fit)*:
Place 90-Second Rule™ reminder sticker on car dashboard; book next Friday's dinner and play; practice and use Breathe Like a Baby™ and The Palm Tree Tool™ when in loud confrontation.

Possible Relationship Key People *(add, edit, or delete as you see fit)*:
Minister; priest; marriage counselor; in-laws; parents; children; work associates; best friends; other relatives; bosses at work; former spouses or mates; friends; and so forth.

Rate your Relationship S.C.O.R.E.® Level:
(1 to 10 with 10 being high)

S.   C.   O.   R.   E.

___   ___   ___   ___   ___

CHAPTER 21

Your Parenting Arena

This Arena is tough, challenging, and, at times, extremely difficult. Welcome to the "awesome" and highly rewarding Parent Arena. I know. I'm also a dad.

Over thirty years ago, I remember driving home with my newborn daughter from the hospital. It seems like yesterday. Days before I had purchased a new VCR, which came with an operating manual with diagrams and detailed instructions. There was even a warranty. The hospital, however, gave no such manual for my infant daughter. Now what do I do?

There was no guide provided for assisting my helpless child for living a life of simplicity, balance, and abundance. None. In fact, there were no instructions for the care and maintenance of my little bundle of joy. All I received was a "Good luck!" from the hospital staff as I drove home well below the speed limit with my hands at 10 and 2 on the steering wheel.

My daughter needed more than a manual. She needed a life blueprint for being her genuine, authentic best self. Where's the blueprint for living? Where's the blueprint for parenting? When do I teach her about being positive? When and how do I explain goal-setting? How do I train her to focus on what she wants and avoid thinking about what she doesn't want? When do I let her fail so the lessons learned will be indelibly etched for a lifetime? What about the concepts of risk and reward and the inevitable need to know and understand supply and demand? How about self-discipline? What's too much? What's too little? How do I help her navigate life's challenges while keeping her optimism intact? Am I overthinking this?

When I instantly became a role model as a parent, I thought, "What do I need to change or adjust in my life in order to more positively influence my kid? Do I raise her like my parents raised me? Or should she be raised like her mother's parents raised her? Or is it the opposite or a combination of the two of us?"

From an early age, my daughter was a challenge when she didn't get her way. Did she learn that in her formative years from birth to five? Probably. When reality didn't meet her expectations, she would throw a tantrum on the tennis court. She has stormed out of the room when not getting her way, even ramming her hand in anger through a glass door. After multiple stitches, she was still angry. This is my kid! What's up with that?

Over three decades later, my daughter is a grown, independent, married woman working as a registered nurse in one of the busiest trauma centers in the country. She handles life and death situations every day. In fact, within months of working her first job, she called me at 2 a.m., after bringing a woman back from death's door to tell me, "Dad, I saved my first life." We both instantly cried on the phone and then she had to hang up to attend her patient.

I'm so proud of my child. She is calm, cool, and poised in the most serious situations one can encounter. It only took her twenty-three years to master it. And it was worth every bit of my frustration, impatience, disappointment, and even dismay. **Colby (Fannin) Sanford**, you're so awesome!

No more getting angry when things don't go her way. She is now a world-class decision-maker at the highest level. Despite her not knowing it, there was a life blueprint and now that she's aware, she's still using it for her new life and future.

Here's another example. **John Buck** is a former Major League Baseball player and All-Star. He had a lot of gas left in his professional baseball tank, but he abruptly packed it in and retired. Why would he throw away the remaining years of his career? His kids are the answer. "I need to be with my kids!" exclaimed John.

As one of my favorite clients, John decided that his onsite and in-home parenting skills (coupled with his great wife and mom, Brooke) were needed to develop his children into world-class decision makers and help them achieve their genuine, authentic best selves. Was it worth turning down millions of dollars and professional adulation? Absolutely.

Kudos to All-Star parents, John & Brooke Buck

There is one Life Arena that directly impacts the collective future of a community, state, or nation. It is the Parenting Arena. This part of your life can mold the next generations of individuals by facilitating high standards of principles, values, and morals. This Arena sets in motion how every culture evolves.

The family unit in America (which contains the Parenting Arena) has unfortunately eroded over the last twenty years. Today, families eat alone, rush to and from children's schedules, think about work during family dinners, overly protect children or let them fend for themselves, disregard formal manners, sleep irregular hours, yell, berate one another, and above all else, DO NOT communicate openly, honestly, and fairly with one another.

It's time to get the Parenting Arena in the Zone. This is a potential place of harmony, love, peace, purpose, and learning. Parents guide the family unit and this is where values are taught and principles of successful living are set. It is the one forum that can help your children evolve into their authentic, genuine best selves.

Your Parenting Blueprint

The following Visions, Big Rocks, Tasks, and Key People have been acquired from The Blueprint of thousands of clients. Place strategic timelines for each of the following and incorporate them within your overall generic calendar. Your children are worth the time investment.

Possible Parenting Visions *(add, edit, or delete as you see fit)***:**

▶ Develop world-class decision maker
▶ Develop my child into his or her authentic, genuine, best self
▶ Coach my kid to greatness
▶ Develop a productive global citizen
▶ Help my child's dreams come true
▶ Develop positive self-esteem

Possible Parenting Big Rocks *(add, edit, or delete as you see fit)***:**

▶ Improve manners
▶ Instill self-discipline
▶ Be firm with punishments
▶ Help around the house
▶ Earn extra income
▶ Guide better nutrition
▶ Eliminate swearing
▶ Maximize concentration
▶ Build positive self-esteem
▶ Toilet train
▶ Get up happy
▶ Go to bed happy
▶ Develop coping skills (when reality doesn't meet expectations)
▶ Help them find their passion
▶ Assist in maximizing grades
▶ Help select the right college
▶ Teach my kid how to relax
▶ Find extracurricular activities

- ▶ Select private school
- ▶ Teach risk and reward principle
- ▶ Teach supply and demand principle

Possible Parenting Tasks *(add, edit or delete as you see fit)***:** Research potential colleges; eliminate all swearing in the house, starting with Dad; set wake-up times and bedtimes; shop with nutrition in mind; eliminate all junk food purchases; act happy every morning; research pros and cons of private schools; research all sports coaches; be aware of all children's self-deprecating behaviors.

Possible Parenting Key People *(add, edit, or delete as you see fit)***:** Teachers; instructors; peer group; grandparents; godparents; aunts and uncles; babysitters; nanny; cousins; sports coach; professional athletes; actors and entertainers; best friends; Mom; Dad; stepparents; life coach; counselors; psychologist; psychiatrist; and so on.

These Key People can have influence on your ability to parent and the overall mindset of your child. With your child's self-esteem, confidence, and belief vulnerable and at risk (especially if they're young), the people they associate with are crucial for their well-being.

Rate your Parenting S.C.O.R.E.® Level:
(1 to 10 with 10 being high)

S.   C.   O.   R.   E.

___   ___   ___   ___   ___

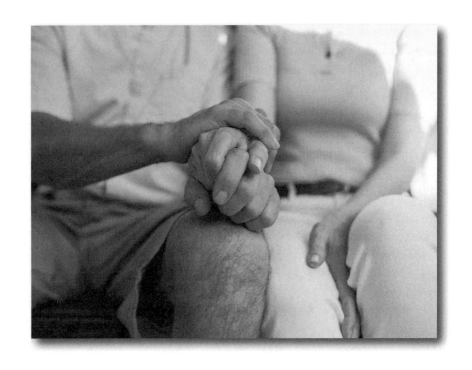

CHAPTER 22

Your Son/Daughter Arena

Eric is a son. His seasonal business had been thriving and his busy season was now upon him. Unfortunately, his father was failing in health and needed to leave the small apartment he had set up near his son. Soon this small business owner's mind totally shifted to his dad, who had to enter the hospital. "I need to help my father," thought Eric. Many of us have been in this situation. You do what you need to do.

Eventually, the hospital had to release his dad because he needed long-term, round-the-clock care. Caregivers and nursing homes were interviewed and the emergency quest was under way. Simultaneously, Eric's bookkeeper's calculations were off, his sales were down, and a few employees suddenly left him without notice. Goodbye, Zone performer.

One day your parents coach you and in time you need to coach them.

Steve is a son. His father drinks too much and often can be inebriated in public. The ambitious son has a serious challenge. Everyone knows this. At his tennis tournaments, dear ol' Dad can be overly nice, obtrusive, mean, abrupt, boisterous, loud, and obnoxious (all within minutes). The pressure on this young college student-athlete client is evident. He is learning to deal with it. He Re-Boots™ and visualizes peace and harmony, even though his dad remains a volatile variable.

In his last tournament with his dad prowling courtside, this great server couldn't buy a first serve. Stress had backed up like a toilet and the overflow onto his tennis game was crippling. How will he cope? The S.C.O.R.E.® System has been his lifeline and mental refuge. His personal blueprint is slowly turning into reality. With persistence and extreme optimism, this son will prevail.

Mary was a great daughter. She loved both her parents with all her heart. When her elderly father fell ill and eventually passed away, the family was devastated. This loss especially impacted Mary's mother. Almost immediately, Mom slipped into depression and as the "only child" daughter that her parents had coached and guided for decades, she was now forced to coach and guide her mom. This role-reversal has been a psychological, financial, and physical hardship.

This Life Arena is all about the thoughts between you and the person or people that raised you. This is typically a parent or parents, but can also be a guardian or guardians, stepparent, foster parents, or other family members.

You love them but you don't always agree. The emotional bonds with the people that raised you can cause amazing friendships over time, but they can easily unravel and even trip up the ultimate Zone performer.

The Key People in this Life Arena are typically your parents. They coached you in your formative years. You probably rebelled in your teenage years from their authority. You wanted independence, but maybe not the responsibility and accountability. Soon you went away to school and moved out of their house. You finally embarked on your independent life. As your parents continue to coach you, they can begin to rub you the wrong way. You may have gotten frustrated or lost patience. Even though you will always be their son or daughter, you now have a life of your own.

Finally, you wake up and realize that your parents need you more than you need them. This drastic role reversal is difficult at first. This is especially true with mothers and daughters and fathers and sons.

Your parents can remain the coaches for parenting their grandchildren or helping resolve your marital issues. However, the tables will turn. It happens when you need to advise them on what to do with their home. Do they sell? Do they refinance? It may occur with their health. You have to constantly remind them to take their medications. Driving a car will eventually become a point of contention when Mom becomes a danger to herself and others on the road.

Many sons and daughters are facing this transition now. This coaching reversal can be traumatic and highly sensitive and emotional. Placing a parent in a senior living community is one of the toughest chores for a son or daughter.

The bottom line is this: They loved in a way they knew how. They parented like they were parented or they rebelled and parented the opposite. They still loved even though they may not have showed it like your best friend's parents. They sacrificed time, money, and energy. The odds are that many of their relationship arguments and disagreements revolved around you.

Honor thy mother and father.

Your Son/Daughter Blueprint

The following Visions, Big Rocks, Tasks, and Key People have been acquired from The Blueprint of thousands of clients. Place strategic timelines for each of the following and incorporate them within your overall generic calendar. Your parents are worth this time investment as you develop this Life Arena from a son or daughter perspective.

Possible Son/Daughter Visions (add, edit, or delete as you see fit): Help parents live great lives; facilitate shared vision; help Mom (Dad) start a new life; help Mom and/or Dad retire with dignity and abundance; help parents' dreams come true.

Possible Son/Daughter Big Rocks (add, edit, or delete as you see fit): Guide parents to create personal will; help with estate plan; move to better place; weigh health care options; organize parents' home; spend weekly quality time; plan family reunion; bolster positive self-esteem; purchase new smart TV.

Possible Son/Daughter Tasks (add, edit, or delete as you see fit): Research and hire new attorney; research healthcare plan pros and cons; visit parents every Friday afternoon; book Ritter Park for reunion; paint parents' front porch; memorialize parents' conversations about their past; compliment daily; research smart TVs; research potential living arrangements.

Possible Son/Daughter Key People (add, edit, or delete as you see fit): Parents' friends; parents' siblings; grandchildren; neighbors; former co-workers; my siblings.

Rate your Son/Daughter S.C.O.R.E.® Level:
(1 to 10 with 10 being high)

S.	C.	O.	R.	E.
—	—	—	—	—

CHAPTER 23

Your Sibling Arena

If you are a brother or sister, then the Sibling Arena is an integral part of The Blueprint. Blood is thicker than water. Many clients, however, have disconnects with their siblings. One small business owner client doesn't communicate with his brother. Ever. Others are at odds with their brothers and sisters because words and deeds from the past cannot be forgiven. I understand this although I'm an only child.

It was a dreary, cold March afternoon and the ride in the backseat was uncomfortable. I was confused. I was angry. I was overcome with sadness for a multitude of reasons. I was fifteen years old and I was not alone in the large Cadillac.

My paternal grandfather, **David Crockett Fannin,** was lying at peace in a coffin in front of us. No one spoke as we followed the hearse to the gravesite. I was sitting between James and Claude Fannin. They were brothers. My Uncle Claude stared straight ahead with an expressionless gaze, while my Dad had his head in his hands. "You both are wrong," I blurted out, breaking the deafening silence. "I'm ashamed to be a Fannin. For my entire life, both of you stubborn men haven't spoken to each other."

Was it a grudge? No one ever knew the real story of why my Dad and uncle stopped talking to each other. We believe it was over money. No family members would ever discuss it. I never saw or spoke to my cousins. I wasn't allowed.

Angrily I continued my pent-up rant, "And now you both go in silence to bury your father, my grandfather. You should be ashamed. This is ridiculous! This is wrong! It is NOT acceptable!"

You could feel the emotion as we left the car and walked to my grandfather's resting place. With the minister speaking as David Crockett Fannin was lowered into the ground, I witnessed a miracle. No words were spoken, but my father and uncle slowly held hands. We all prayed. We all cried.

Negative thoughts that produce anger, jealousy, resentment, disdain, scorn, condescension, or ill will are physically and mentally unhealthy. They are too burdensome for the champion. The successful person swiftly says, "I'm sorry." "Forgive me." "I forgive you." "Let's work this out."

THE BLUEPRINT

Negative thoughts over time will take their toll. They slow you down. They attract what you don't want. They distract you. They keep you tethered to the very thing that upset you. You become the victim. You become the prisoner of the past, draining hope and positivity. These thoughts can eventually manifest themselves into a negative reality.

A few years ago, I convinced a good friend to make peace with his sister. "She is so deceitful," he lamented. They had been at odds with no communication between them. "I will never speak to her again," he promised. There was anger. There was resentment. Finally with my encouragement, he approached his only sibling and they bonded. They straightened out their differences. Soon after, his sister died. There were no regrets. "I talked to her every day the last few months of her life and am glad we found common ground," he confessed. My friend found peace and understanding. He has closure.

We all have people challenges and even conflicts. We all have disappointments with the ones we like and especially love. Let go of the story. It's the story that fuels our emotional unrest. Once the story is eliminated from your mind, nothing can power the negative feelings. Move forward.

Let go of the negative past.

Most siblings have been hurt by the actions or words of their brother or sister. Perhaps your brother criticized your choice of a significant other. I saw this play out with a MLB pitcher and his brother. They did everything together until a new girlfriend entered the scene. She demanded more of my client's time and he readily obliged. Soon, jealousy of a potential wife led to his only sibling's malice and anger.

Maybe your sibling didn't believe in your talent. Maybe he or she still sees and treats you as the baby sister even though you now make more money than he or she does. Possibly his or her consistent and blatant "holier than thou" attitude finally took its toll. These psychological wounds can penetrate your soul. They can overrun your mind like weeds in a garden. They can produce feelings of revenge, hatred, bitterness, and anger. Forgiveness, however, can set you free. By embracing forgiveness, you can also embrace the feelings of peace and hope.

180

Forgiveness is the process of ending resentment or anger as a result of a perceived offense, difference, or mistake, or ceasing to demand punishment or restitution.

With forgiveness, you make a decision to let go of resentment and thoughts of revenge. It took my father a lifetime to release the story of his past that had fueled his negative emotions. The act that hurt or offended him remained a part of his life. He even tried to pass these feelings on to his only son...ME. After forgiveness entered my father's psyche and negativity lessened its grip on him, it helped him move forward. Forgiveness even led to his feelings of understanding, empathy, and compassion for my uncle, the one who he believed had hurt him.

Know that forgiveness doesn't minimize or justify the wrong. You can forgive your sibling without excusing their act. Forgiving, however, can make way for peace. It can lead to lower blood pressure, reduction of stress, increased new healthy relationships, decreased symptoms of depression, and a lowered risk of alcohol and drug abuse.

Forgiveness is a commitment to a process of change.

If you are struggling to reconcile with a sibling, decide now to:

- Extend an olive branch of peace.
- Forgive swiftly. Do not allow lingering negativity.
- Forgive often. Make this a habit.
- Seek forgiveness, although it may never arrive.
- Move forward with hope and positivity.
- Learn from the past, then bury it and refuse to dig it up again.
- Find common ground and together leverage its power.
- Learn to say, "I'm sorry," "Forgive me," and "I forgive you"— and mean it.
- Be honest with yourself and others.
- Monitor your thoughts for feelings of being a victim or judge.
- Replace all negative images, words, and deeds with a positive, future vision.
- Use the S.C.O.R.E.® Success System to live in the moment.

How powerful is forgiveness? It releases the negative past and opens a revitalized energy source that can pave an amazing future of simplicity and balance.

Make amends. Bury the hatchet. Make peace. Pick up the phone. Look them in the eye. Control the situation or circumstance by making the first move. Empty the anger from your heart. Sever the tethered thoughts that keep you connected to the negative transgression or offense. Move forward.

My father and uncle finally became good friends after they left my grandfather's gravesite. They spoke often. They met often. They forgave each other. I still can see them holding hands, as if they were kids again. They were brothers. They loved each other. They embraced forgiveness.

Siblings know the good, bad, and ugly of their brothers and sisters. There are secrets. There are old wounds. Resentments, jealousies, and distrust can directly impact the way you act and interact with sibling family members.

Most importantly, there are opportunities of positive growth. Of course, love conquers all. Create the direction of this Life Arena below.

Your Sibling Blueprint

The following Visions, Big Rocks, Tasks, and Key People have been acquired from The Blueprint of thousands of clients. Place strategic timelines for each of the following and incorporate them within your overall generic calendar. Your siblings are worth the time investment.

Possible Sibling Visions *(add, edit, or delete as you see fit)*: Best sibling possible; family MVP; sibling leader; mental, physical, and spiritual leader.

Possible Sibling Big Rocks *(add, edit, or delete as you see fit)*: Help brother financially; upgrade sibling interaction; communicate weekly; follow siblings on Facebook; plan family reunion; help sister through divorce; know sibling's dreams; know my nieces and nephews.

Possible Sibling Tasks *(add, edit, or delete as you see fit)*: Loan brother $1,000; research divorce attorney; have lunch Tuesday with sister; place nieces' and nephews' birthdays in calendar; introduce brother to my banker; call sister on Friday; check Facebook.

Possible Sibling Key People *(add, edit, or delete as you see fit)*: Brothers and/or sisters; parents; grandparents; guardians; stepparents; sibling friends; siblings' spouses; nieces; nephews; siblings' co-workers; neighbors.

These people can have influence over many aspects of your life. They witness all of your positive qualities and attributes, but they also get to experience your faults, foibles, and negative tendencies.
Rate each sibling's S.C.O.R.E.® Level. Which S.C.O.R.E.® component could you help him or her bolster? After this is done, rate your own S.C.O.R.E.® Level regarding how you are as a brother or sister.

Rate your Sibling S.C.O.R.E.® Level:
(1 to 10 with 10 being high)

S.	C.	O.	R.	E.
___	___	___	___	___

CHAPTER 24

Your Personal Finance Arena

"I can't afford it," she complained. "We'll run out of money if we live to be eighty-years old," forecast a fearful spouse. "If we lose our insurance, we're screwed with Amy's illness," cried a loving parent. "How can I get a place of my own in a warmer climate?" queried the hopeful graduate. "How do I pay for three college students at the same time?" says a concerned parent. "I need more income!" an over-spender barks.

Your Personal Finance Arena represents the cash in your pocket, equity in your home, and value of your stock portfolio, 401(k), and everything else involving your money. This Life Arena is crucial for your overall wellbeing. It can have a positive or negative impact on all of the other Arenas in your life.

Financial woes can directly interfere with your Relationship, Self, Job, and Parenting Arenas. Tension over finances can be crippling and cause emotion to override reason. Restlessness, worry, anxiety, and fear about money can impact all positive moods in a negative way. Personal finances can weigh heavily on your mind and the preoccupation with money can and probably will tarnish the other Arenas in your life.

On the flipside, money can provide an incredible quality of life, including simplicity and balance. How are your personal finances? Is everything in order?

Money...Money...Money. You want it. You need it. And you have it...at least for a little while. When you get a crisp $100 bill and place the newly minted Benjamin in your wallet, it feels good. Stack a wad of these big bills in your wallet or purse and you feel great. However, as soon as you break it and the leftover change trickles back into your wallet, it's invariably GONE. It won't be long until the entire $100 has disappeared. Poof! Vanished into thin air.

It's NOT about how much money you make, but how much you keep.

Never have we spent so much and saved so little. We spend and borrow too much. In the long run, it spells trouble for individuals and the nation. Most of us go on spending happily until the reality of hard times arrives.

Champions prepare for the worst while expecting the best.

Disaster with your job, health, home, car, or even an economic recession can strike without warning. Assets and income will then drop and the danger zone of no cash will become real.

Where's Ben Franklin when we need him? "**If you would be wealthy, think of saving as well as getting,**" our forefather advised. There are many factors for poor savings. So what? It's over and done. Let's not look back. It is what it is. Let's go forward. Here's a few tips.

- ▶ Make an investment in visualizing the money you want. See it. See the raise. See the extra sales. See your profits. See it often. See it before sleep. Believe and expect to have an abundance of money.
- ▶ Take ten to fifteen percent and hide it from every paycheck. Do it simultaneously with your deposit. Park it in a low-risk place.
- ▶ If you own a business, pay yourself first. I know...I've violated this tenet before. No more.
- ▶ Cut spending by twenty percent if possible. Stay home. Eat in. Travel less. Use coupons. (Wow...my friends never thought they'd read this from me.) Why pay more when you can get it for less? Why?
- ▶ Review your bills. I've found so many mistakes with bank statements, credit card statements, and grocery store receipts. I never used to look. I do now.
- ▶ Pay cash. Use a debit card. Don't use a credit card unless you pay it off each month. Period.

▸ Stop helping others at the expense of yourself and your family. Stop it. Say, NO!

▸ Now is a good time to invest if you have the available cash. An uncertain future presents many opportunities. Project the world five years from now. What will we need? Real estate is always good for the long haul. Research. Research. Research.

▸ Start a business only if it fills you with passion. Control your vision and goals. Sharpen your self-discipline. Only go for it if your heart is in it for more than the money. However, you still need to think about money, as it's the lifeblood of every company.

▸ Risk wisely. Invest no more than fifteen percent of your portfolio in risky investments. Be prepared to have this cash extracted and lost from your overall wealth. Detach from any negative feelings if this happens. Be wise. Be cautiously bold.

My friends know I'm NOT frugal. So why am I providing these tips? I guess my beloved, Depression-era grandmother is looking down and nodding her head at me.

Life is more than money, that's for sure. But life is getting longer. I see me living to 125. Why not? Will I work that long? I hope. Will my money last that long? Hmmm...I don't know. I believe it will.

Think rich. Be wise. Minimize your risk. Get your money in the Zone. Money matters!

Your Personal Finance Blueprint

The following Visions, Big Rocks, Tasks, and Key People have been acquired from The Blueprint of thousands of clients. Place strategic timelines for each of the following and incorporate them within your overall generic calendar. Your personal finances are worth the time investment.

Possible Personal Finance Visions *(add, edit, or delete as you see fit)*:
- Financial independence
- $1,000,000 net worth
- $5,000,000 net worth
- $5,000,000 diversified portfolio
- Retire independently wealthy at age 40
- Retire independently wealthy at age 50
- Retire independently wealthy at age 60
- Wealthy philanthropist

Possible Personal Finance Big Rocks *(add, edit, or delete as you see fit)*:
- Save $100 monthly
- Save $500 monthly
- Max-out 401(k)
- $200,000 college fund
- Diversify portfolio (gold, real estate, stocks, bonds, cash)
- Buy $25,000 in gold
- Purchase rental income-producing real estate ($1M)
- Save twenty percent of net income
- Purchase franchise
- Create or update my will
- Hire financial planner
- Hire CPA
- Hire tax attorney
- Create estate plan
- Increase life insurance

- Invest $100,000 in REIT
- Create family budget
- Refinance home
- Purchase vacation home
- Lease autos
- Expense home office
- Pay myself first

Possible Personal Finance Tasks *(add, edit, or delete as you see fit)*: Organize direct deposit; research financial planners; meet bank manager; research new CPA; purchase QuickBooks online; meet insurance broker Tuesday; order home appraisal; enroll in 401(k).

Possible Personal Finance Key People *(add, edit, or delete as you see fit)*: Financial advisor; stockbroker; insurance broker; attorney; accountant; spouse; friends; banker; realtor; financial blogger; host of finance TV shows; bookkeeper; and so on.

These people can have influence over your retirement; financial independence; savings accounts; net worth; stock portfolio; stress; anxiety; worry; fear; overall happiness; and so forth.

Rate your Personal Finance S.C.O.R.E.® Level:
(1 to 10 with 10 being high)

S.	C.	O.	R.	E.
___	___	___	___	___

CHAPTER 25

Your Friends Arena

Sharing life experiences with good friends brings life to its fullest. Friendship leverages these unique and one-of-a-kind social occurrences.

The Friends Arena contains your close friends, a large quantity of their thoughts, and your thoughts regarding them. Your friends are the mirror image of yourself. Birds of a feather flock together. These are your friends. Moving from someone you met to an acquaintance to a friend, good friend or best friend is the process. As you develop your Friends Arena, place people in this part of your life that are ONLY good friends.

What is a good friend? Here are qualifications. Add, delete, or edit this list as you see fit.

A good friend...

- Accepts you as you are. They understand your flaws and good points and still count you as a good friend.
- Thinks and says positive things about you when you're not there.
- Arrives to help when you're in a crisis or predicament.
- Remembers and celebrates the milestones in your life.
- Celebrates your successes.
- Tells you the truth even if it's difficult.
- Shares their most intimate secrets.
- Keeps secrets and honors confidential information.
- Always makes you laugh and smile.
- Has your back unconditionally.
- Supports your choices in all your Arenas even when they disagree.
- Tells it like it is.
- Knows how to make you laugh.
- Makes you a better person.
- Becomes a part of your family.
- Bolsters your confidence and overall optimism.
- Sacrifices time, energy, and sometimes money for your benefit.
- Makes your life more fun and enjoyable.
- Has a relaxing and calming presence.
- Is liked by your mom and dad.

Are you a good friend?

Can you help your friends reach their Visions and Big Rocks? What can you do for them? Do you know their dreams? Do you know their children's dreams? Good friends will love you unconditionally. Even if you're not always your best, they still stand by your side. They love you regardless of your blemishes, scars, and warts. As a good friend, you reciprocate without anything being said. It is these relationships that make both parties better.

Pam and Tracy became friends in high school. They were inseparable! But, as life moved forward, their lives took different paths. Pam married a truck driver, had three children, and moved from the expensive suburb she grew up in to a blue-collar town nearby. Tracy, on the other hand, went to college and graduate school. She became a high-powered management consultant and flew all over the world, meeting people and experiencing new things. Every year, they got together for a "best friends' weekend." It was during these times that the friendship felt as comfortable and warm as when they were in high school. Although Pam struggled with finances, she was so happy that Tracy was experiencing financial success. And while Tracy was lonely and missed having a life partner and children, she was happy that her best friend Pam had a life filled with love. Instead of being jealous of each other, Pam and Tracy let their friendship bring out their best qualities.

Sharing in a good friend's success is an honor and you support them even if their success moves them to a different geographical location or socio-economic status. Good friendships continue to evolve regardless of good or tough times.

Your Friends Blueprint

The following Visions, Big Rocks, Tasks, and Key People have been acquired from The Blueprint of thousands of clients. Place strategic timelines for each of the following and incorporate them within your overall generic calendar. Your relationship with your friends is worth it.

Possible Friends Visions *(add, edit, or delete as you see fit)*: Best friend possible; mental, physical, and spiritual bond; friend's MVP; exemplary friend; great friend; unconditional friendship.

Possible Friends Big Rocks *(add, edit, or delete as you see fit)*: Learn more about your friend's past; monthly girls' night out; monthly boys' night out; help your friend through divorce; know your friend's dreams and visions; ask better questions; listen proactively; help your friend move; help your friend with their parents' finances; organize Christmas trip; invite to family Thanksgiving; buy birthday gift.

Possible Friends Tasks *(add, edit, or delete as you see fit)*: Clear Saturday for your friend's move; book restaurant for Friday night; book hotel for December; meet friend's parents on Friday.

Possible Friends Key People *(add, edit, or delete as you see fit)*: friend's friends; friend's spouse; friend's children; friend's parents; my parents; my siblings; my children; friend's co-workers; friend's neighbors.

Rate your Friends S.C.O.R.E.® Level:
(1 to 10 with 10 being high)

S.   C.   O.   R.   E.

___   ___   ___   ___   ___

CHAPTER 26

Other Possible Life Arenas

Although there are no rules to how many Life Arenas can be in The Blueprint, it's still recommended to have no more than ten. "Less is more" applies. Here are some optional Life Arenas.

Your Hobby Arena

"Last year, I saw 100 stage plays by volunteering to be an usher. My hobby has kept me active since my retirement. I love it," a senior hobbyist recalled.

"I love to knit. It gives me so much enjoyment and sense of accomplishment. Plus, when I get in the Zone, nothing else matters," rejoices a knitter.

"Fishing is my getaway. Lost on a pond or river is heaven for me. I am a fisherman," he laughed out loud.

This Arena contains your thoughts about scuba diving, knitting, backgammon, chess, poker, weight lifting, traveling, modeling, volunteering, art and crafts, painting, or other activities that give you pleasure and enjoyment. You perform in this Arena when you have spare time. Your hobby, unfortunately, takes the backseat to many other Arenas.

The Hobby Arena is a great refuge from your toughest and most challenging Arenas. Focusing on your hobby can lower your stress level and elevate your level of enjoyment. Finding the Zone readily makes this Arena attractive for investing more time and energy. Other fellow hobbyists can form a passionate support group that validates the time, money and energy you spend.

Your Home Arena

"I can't believe we spent $22,000 on plumbing and wiring and you can't even see it," bemoaned a homeowner. "We need a new deck before someone kills themselves," cries a needy owner. "You promised me a new kitchen, not a bass boat! Really...a bass boat?" yells a disgruntled wife. "I'm getting my own job. I'm sick of your promises!" she said boldly. Your abode can be rented or owned, but either way it's home and emotions and cash reside here.

At home, you can let down your hair and be yourself. If only your walls could talk. They would reveal your worries, concerns, hopes, and fears. Home matters for so many reasons. Most, however, like their home to be nice and inviting for friends, family, and guests.

Your Home Arena is typically your biggest emotional and financial investment and continuing expense. It can have a tremendous impact on your S.C.O.R.E.® Level.

This Arena impacts your Relationship, Parenting, Personal Finance, and Self Arenas. Because you spend an inordinate amount of time, energy, and money here, it has a major influence on your overall mindset.

Today, more people are improving their homes than ever. The "fix it yourself" revolution has arrived. Many people are seeking warmer weather or dual homes to take advantage of these conditions. Downsizing has also become prevalent with tiny homes (750 square feet or less) becoming an option.

Your Home Arena revolves around your current home, second home, new home, overall home vision, improvement goals, and the tasks. It also houses the mental interior design needed to turn your dream home or homes into reality.

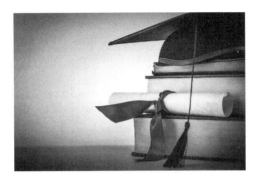

Your Academic or School Arena

We spend an inordinate amount of time, effort, and money in school. For some, time spent in school has been twenty-five to thirty-five percent of their lives. From a kindergarten class to a PhD program, our education is crucial for making major life changes. The higher your education, the more options you'll have. The well-educated have more geographical options and income opportunities as well as a potential upgrade of friends and associates. This was a major Life Arena and it still is for all current students.

This Arena demands Zone performances. Test taking under a time constraint creates the pressure to attract or repel the Zone. The Academic Arena requires your full attention to be successful.

Your "Other Family" Arena

Sometimes your "other family" members play a significant role in your life. These are family members with whom you interact on a regular basis. They can play a major role in your confidence, self-esteem, and overall wellbeing, especially if you are estranged from your parents or sibling.

PART 4

Your Business Blueprint

This section addresses your business, career, or job. You'll find information on leadership, management, sales, and being an entrepreneur.

CHAPTER 27

Your Job Arena

This Life Arena is all about your job. It is your occupation, trade, profession, career, or employment. Management, sales, and small business ownership will be addressed later.

"Dad, can I have a dollar?"

My father replied with a laugh, "I don't have a dollar. You'll have to earn your own dollar."

"Well, how do I do that?" I asked with the utmost naiveté—the kind that only a seven-year-old can have.

My father looked me in the eye and said, "You can't make a buck until you sell something or do something. That's called a job!"

Dad continued his soliloquy with, "What thing can you sell or do that you really know? Who wants what you sell or do and will they pay for it?

"Okay," was all I answered.

With Dad's monologue replaying in my brain, I walked to the nearby gas station and asked for a job.

The man looked at me and laughed, "Your dad know you're here?"

"No sir," I politely replied.

"Well, I'll pay you ten cents a day to wipe the car windshields. Do you know how?"

I fudged the truth with a short, muffled, "Yessir."

After five attempts that took too long with poor results, he gently fired me. "Jimmy, come back when you're older." I was too short to provide the "something to do" to make a buck. And it would've taken me forever to make a buck. Providing a service was not going to get it done.

A few days later, I was trying my best to help my father wash our old, beat-up Buick. It was 1957 and he wished he had a nicer car. In fact, my Dad wanted to drive a brand new Thunderbird convertible. He dreamed of being behind the wheel of this exquisite automobile.

"Why don't you get that car?" I innocently asked.

"That's a rich man's car," he replied.

"How do you get rich?" I pondered aloud.

"Forget rich, I can't even get a job," exclaimed my father.

"Me neither," I thought. I didn't tell him because I wasn't allowed down at the gas station. Of course, he later found out anyway.

We lived in Morehead, Kentucky, and everybody knew everybody's business. However, in just a few minutes, I was about to learn all I needed to know about getting a job and even more importantly...how to get rich.

My father broke it down like this. "Look across the fence, Jimmy. That's where the money is. Mr. Caudill owns the lumberyard in town and everybody needs lumber. He's rich. We're poor. Everyone on this side of the fence rents a house. Everyone on the other side owns a house. If you want to have money, you need to go where the money is. The money is over there."

"Hmmm." And that's all I needed to know.

The next day I took my Radio Flyer red wagon and filled it with apples I found on the ground by a small orchard down by the creek. Then I knocked on Mr. Caudill's door, and when he answered I said, "My name is Jimmy Fannin, would you like to buy some apples?"

Stunned by my diminutive size and enormous bravado he asked, "How much?" And with all of the courage I could muster I said, "You can have them all for $1." He immediately left the doorway and came back with a buck. My first sale was made. Of course, Mr. Caudill would later laugh while telling the story of buying his own apples from his orchard from Jimmy Fannin for a dollar.

Capitalism at its finest. This is probably how Wall Street got started. Don't they still do it like this?

Later, my mother was reading a copy of *Life* magazine. When she finished, she threw it in the wastebasket.

"Is it still good?" I asked.

"What do you mean Jimmy?" queried Mom.

"Is it still good to read by someone else?"

"Absolutely," replied my unsuspecting mother. In fact, she had just helped launch my second business.

The next day, I went to the rich side of the fence and asked the rich if I could have their old magazines after they read them. All said yes. I collected them like a trash man and loaded them in my red wagon. Then I went to the poor side and took orders for weekly and monthly deliveries of the most popular periodicals. Of course, I sold them for half price and delivered them about a week after the rich had read them.

I controlled the supply and there was plenty of demand.

The United States unemployment rate has millions of people out of work. Our economy is shaky and the future is looking more and more uncertain. There are plenty of reasons why we are in this situation. Look at our country's economic state from your perspective. Understand your personal situation with its unique conditions and circumstances. Here are some points to ponder:

- All kids need a job. That's right! Start them early. It could be mowing the lawn or cleaning the basement. Teach them how to think. Teach them about money. Teach them the basics of making money, getting a job, and developing a career.
- You make money by selling a product or a service. Simple enough!
- You get rich by selling a whole lot of inexpensive things or a smaller amount of really expensive things. Hopefully, you can sell a whole lot of expensive things.
- It's not the gross sales that make you rich. It's the amount of money you keep after the expenses have been paid. Okay... that's Business 101.
- Whoever takes the most risk in money and time should get the biggest rewards. Period.
- To get and keep a job you need to understand that you will be hired or are hired to impact profit for a company. Income comes in and expenses go out. Hopefully, there is a profit left over that warrants the sacrifice of time and money for the owner. That's how you keep a job and hopefully get a raise. Which part of the equation (income or expenses) does your job impact? Maybe it's both. Whichever it is, maximize it. Make yourself invaluable. Make yourself indispensable. Help the owner make money.
- From a job you can learn the pros and cons of business on another person's dime. Pay attention. Be aware. Not a bad deal if you ever want to start your own business.
- If there is great demand for a product or service and the supply of it is small, then the price will rise. The opposite is also true.

- Experts make more money than non-experts. This is true especially when the expertise is needed. If you have a job, know, befriend, and learn from the experts.
- Show another man how to make money and he doesn't mind giving you a little money. I've made a fortune with this concept.

How do you get a job? How do you get rich? Go sell Mr. Caudill a lot of apples in your Radio Flyer red wagon.

Your Job Blueprint

The following Visions, Big Rocks, Tasks, and Key People have been placed on The Blueprint from thousands of executives, workers, and employees from fifty industries. Place strategic timelines for each of the following and incorporate them within your overall business calendar.

Possible Job Visions *(add, edit, or delete as you see fit)*:

- President of company
- C-Suite elevation
- Promotion to next level
- Ownership
- Equity position
- Partner
- Department head
- Division head
- Industry change
- Career change
- Entrepreneurship
- Financial security
- Medical benefits
- Establish career

Possible Job Big Rocks *(add, edit, or delete as you see fit)*:

- Expert knowledge and experience (be specific)
- Better planning skills
- Time management skills
- Stress management skills
- Leadership skills
- Great communicator
- Expert body language reader
- Better proactive listener
- Industry-specific skills

- Computer skills (be specific)
- $100,000 salary
- Specific salary increase
- More responsibility (be specific)
- Better benefits
- Better working conditions
- Work-life balance
- Less travel or more travel
- Corner office
- Reserved parking

Possible Job Tasks *(add, edit, or delete as you see fit)*: Enroll in law school; hire recruiter; enroll in computer class; enroll in master's program; book golf Saturday tee time with boss; buy new golf clubs; volunteer for corporate 5K race Saturday.

Possible Job Key People *(add, edit, or delete as you see fit)*: Chairman; vice chairman; chief executive officer; chief operating officer; chief financial officer; board member; committee lead; director; owner; president; vice president; division head; department head; general manager; manager; HR specialist; assistant manager; boss; supervisor; foreman; team leader; co-worker; executive coach; spouse; subordinates; clients; prospects; and so on.

These people can have influence over compensation; daily performance, confidence; self-esteem; optimism; relaxation; enjoyment; passion; worry; anxiety; fear; promotions; bonuses; transfers; or firing.

Rate your Job S.C.O.R.E.® Level:
(1 to 10 with 10 being high)

S.	C.	O.	R.	E.
—	—	—	—	—

CHAPTER 28

Your Management Arena

"My team is so diverse in intellect, drive, initiative, and even geographically. We need to be on the same page," manager **Julie McAllister** revealed.

Julie was an HR manager for an international corporation. She was positive, direct, and open-minded about inspiring her team. She retained me to help. When I was introduced to her team, she made it clear the information they would receive was to be used selfishly for each person. "Take off your corporate hat and be here alone individually with Jim," she proudly stated. After four, ninety-minute sessions, her team began to open up and ask extremely great questions. Julie's initial "divide and conquer" approach to management worked as she later galvanized her diverse team as a holistic energy force against all global competition and for specific, well-defined group projects. Julie manages in the Zone.

Introducing The Blueprint concept brought Julie's team together even more. Soon, they realized their role was so much more than a job and they were more than employees. They became aware they were an integral part of something greater than themselves.

Julie's group (from Poland to the United States and Columbia, and elsewhere) identified each person's responsibility, accountability, and authority. These three factors empowered her team and ignited the problem-solving imagination and creativity her company had needed.

You are a manager, a boss, and a leader. Your Management Arena is complex, as it contains the thoughts and feelings of a lot of other people. This dynamic of managing multiple, simultaneous thoughts that may or may not be in harmony, can prove successful or not. Either way, there will be a lot of stress managing various mindsets with different experience, agendas, skillsets, and intentions.

With the average person having 2,000 to 3,000 thoughts every day, your company cannot expect to use all of them. Even during working hours, a team member's thoughts can change from family to friends to personal matters and back to business within a matter of seconds. However, a company does expect to get the most thoughts of their employees and the most quality of thoughts it can.

Your responsibility is to manage thoughts.

Some workers think about business the full sixteen to seventeen hours of their waking moments. They take their business thoughts home with them. Others leave their thoughts about business at the door as they exit the office. When the big hand's on twelve and the little hand is on five, their work brain slams shut. Closed for the day. Every worker is different.

As manager you must realize that you do not manage people. You manage thoughts. And every thought is a literal action. When a person's thoughts change, their actions change. When actions change, the reaction is set in motion. Actions change, results change, and goals are reached or not reached.

Most senior managements operate from a balance sheet and or a profit and loss (P/L) statement. There are two types of P/L statements:

Dead P/L: This is just looking at the numbers and deducing that they are too high or too low. When you're looking at the line items for income and expenses to see if there is a profit or loss, you are looking at a Dead P/L. You are looking at it from a cold numbers point of view, analyzing it in terms of profit and loss. Most managers look at dead P/L numbers.

Living P/L: In a Living P/L, the sales income of a particular product has to do with the thoughts of the sales personnel, sales support staff, marketing team, supply chain team, manufacturing team, and the thoughts of the customer. These collective thoughts will formulate the sales income. Change the thoughts in these line items, and the numbers will change.

When you look at each line item of income and expense, recognize the thoughts that contribute to that line item. For example, on the expense side of the P/L, if the thoughts of the suppliers who are contributing to that particular line item change, that number can increase or decrease.

By understanding that there are thoughts that run into each line item, you can now begin to change those thoughts. This will start the chain reaction that will change the numbers in your company's P/L statement.

Thoughts must change long before numbers can change.

In the automobile sales industry, for example, a sales team may be high pressure selling—putting the squeeze on people as soon as they walk in the door. As soon as the unwary prospect arrives, three salespersons go on the offensive.

"Good afternoon! What new automobile can I show you?" says the first employee on the scene.

Simultaneously, another salesperson barks in mid-stride, "How are you? We've got some great deals this month" and finally the last sales hawk to arrive beckons, "My name is Bob Johnson and you are...? Joan and Darren, what are you looking for? Let me show you around."

The quantity of thoughts between the salespeople and the prospect has elements of jealousy, envy, trepidation, fear, hunger, passion, honesty, dishonesty, and worry.

Sales will not increase until that sales process changes to a friendlier, comfortable, and relaxed environment that is conducive to purchase. When a salesperson realizes that he or she doesn't sell cars, they motivate people to improve their quality of transportation at a price they can afford, car sales will increase because thoughts have positively changed.

The next time you look at your P/L statement, look at it as a living P/L. Look at it through a different pair of lenses. See the people and the thoughts of the people that are flowing into these line items. Then you can begin to make changes in people's thoughts, and watch the numbers change for the better.

Manage your P/L statement into the Zone, and you'll produce a healthier bottom line.

Your Management Blueprint

The following Visions, Big Rocks, Tasks, and Key People have been placed on The Blueprint from thousands of mangers from fifty industries, as well as managers from sports and other entities. Place strategic timelines for each of the following and incorporate them within your overall business calendar.

Possible Management Visions *(add, edit, or delete as you see fit)*:

▶ Promotion
▶ Company president
▶ Ownership
▶ Equity position
▶ Partner
▶ Department head
▶ Division head
▶ Industry change
▶ Career change
▶ Entrepreneurship
▶ Golden parachute
▶ Retirement
▶ Increased salary (be specific)

Possible Management Big Rocks *(add, edit, or delete as you see fit)*:

▶ Expert knowledge and experience (be specific)
▶ Better planning skills
▶ Expert platform speaker/presenter
▶ Time management skills
▶ Conflict resolution skills
▶ Stress management skills
▶ Leadership skills
▶ Great communicator
▶ Expert body language reader
▶ Better proactive listener
▶ Industry specific skills

▶ Computer skills (be specific)
▶ Stock options
▶ $100,000 salary
▶ $500,000 salary
▶ $1,000,000 gross compensation
▶ Specific salary increase
▶ More responsibility (be specific)
▶ Better benefits
▶ Better working conditions
▶ Work-life balance
▶ Less travel or more travel

Possible Management Tasks *(add, edit, or delete as you see fit)*: Enroll in yoga class Tuesday–Thursday–Saturday; enroll in master's program; research executive coaches; interview administrative assistants; read *The Blueprint*; meet HR re: insurance; book annual conference room; one-on-one with employees; re-model office kitchen; buy *The Blueprint* for team; and so on.

Possible Management Key People *(add, edit, or delete as you see fit)*: Boss; company president; direct reports; board members; co-worker; executive coach; spouse; clients; subordinates; prospects; yoga instructor; public speaking coach; children; and so forth.

These people can have influence over compensation; daily performance; happiness; fulfillment; worry; anxiety; negative stress; promotions or firing.

Rate your Management S.C.O.R.E.® Level:
(1 to 10 with 10 being high)

S.   C.   O.   R.   E.

___   ___   ___   ___   ___

Your Sales Arena

Introducing the sales team in Norway to my S.C.O.R.E.® Success System was a special treat for me. Without question, their training was already the international gold standard and I was there to put the cherry on the top of this already well-baked, sales cake.

Upon arriving at their offices, I was taken to their windowless, packed-to-capacity basement and there I saw every competitor's office printer lined up in rows. As my host walked me down the aisles of machines, he offered little tidbits of knowledge on each product.

"This is a competitor's wireless inkjet, all-in-one printer, copier, and scanner," he bluntly remarked. Ironically, this was not his company's machine.

I thought to myself, "Am I at the wrong company?" Then he stopped at another competitor's color laser, all-in-one printer, copier, scanner, and fax and proceeded to take it apart and check all of its vital parts. "Wow. He is taking this apart like an M16 in army boot camp," I silently thought in awe.

Every salesperson knew every product on the market. They could walk into any office and fix any machine, regardless of the make or model. They not only knew their own product expertly, but they also knew their competitor's product better than their salespeople. I was duly impressed.

Without sales, there is no company. Period. With intense competition and uncertainty this Life Arena is crucial in business.

Champions control their success and in business, success begins with sales. The best of the best sales professionals are in control. Regardless of the situation, condition and or circumstances, these sales champions thrive.

With the Zone mindset of a "purposeful calm," sales champions maneuver the sales process like the best point guard in the NBA guides his offense.

Dedication. Execution. Precision. Tenacity. Resolve. Poise.

No excuses for the champion salesperson. None. Excuses are for non-champions. The economy, fierce competition, unfair business practices, price fixing, or other challenges that the average salesperson complains about **DO NOT** negatively impact the successful sales professional. The best of the best control their sales destiny with no exceptions.

To be successful in the Sales Arena, you must manage your personal energy because with every "No" to a potential sale, a piece of your energy can be extracted. If not checked, energy reserves can become depleted and the "Teeter-Totter Effect™" of performance can arrive. This "up and down" energy flow can cause burnout and great sales personnel avoid this malady.

Be unfazed with a "NO" as you only seek a YES. "Next!" is your battle cry.

Your Sales Blueprint

The following Visions, Big Rocks, Tasks, and Key People have been placed on the personal Blueprint from hundreds of thousands of sales personnel from more than 30 countries and 50 industries. From GE Healthcare, Morgan Stanley, Merrill Lynch, Silhouette Optical and Diamond Resorts International to Mercedes, Toyota, Honda, and Chrysler sales teams, the Sales Blueprint has made each person more money with better work-life balance. Place strategic timelines for each of the following and incorporate them within your overall sales calendar.

Possible Sales Visions *(add, edit, or delete as you see fit)*:
▶ National sales record
▶ Annual sales leader
▶ Regional sales record
▶ Company sales record
▶ Company sales leader
▶ Personal sales record
▶ $10M annual sales
▶ $100M annual sales
▶ Sales manager position
▶ Company president
▶ National product line
▶ Twenty percent market share

Possible Sales Big Rocks *(add, edit, or delete as you see fit)*:
▶ Fifty calls daily
▶ Sixty percent closing ratio
▶ New business suits
▶ Upgrade presentation material
▶ Log info daily into sales force software
▶ Improve public speaking
▶ Learn Prezi presentation software

- ▶ Hire life coach
- ▶ Work-life balance
- ▶ Follow-up calls (within one hour)
- ▶ Create ten-day, thirty-day and ninety-day customer on-boarding process
- ▶ Increase product knowledge (be specific)
- ▶ Increase customer knowledge (be specific)
- ▶ Join sales network
- ▶ Daily LinkedIn activity
- ▶ Learn new closing techniques

Possible Sales Tasks *(add, edit, or delete as you see fit)*: Enroll in a Sales Blueprint™ course; enroll in public speaking class; update database; add pictures to customer database; send holiday cards; book customer tee time for Wednesday; book customer dinner for Thursday; and so on.

Possible Sales Key People *(add, edit or delete as you see fit)*: Boss; co-worker; sales coach; sales manager; life coach; ZoneCoach®; spouse; subordinates; support staff; assistant; clients; prospects; industry net-worker; sales guru; sales blogger; and so forth.

These Key People can have influence over compensation; new sales; sales retention; daily performance; happiness; fear; worry; anxiety; promotions; bonuses; quotas; expenses; or firing.

Rate your Sales S.C.O.R.E.® Level:
(1 to 10 with 10 being high)

S.   C.   O.   R.   E.

___   ___   ___   ___   ___

217

CHAPTER 30

Your Entrepreneur Arena

Regina sells soul food in her small restaurant and her business is booming. Every detail, from the inventory of ribs to the temperature of her cooler, is known. "I see every detail," says Regina with pride. She runs the business with an iron fist and micro-management is her style.

Entrepreneurial businesses require attention to detail. However, without a well-defined Blueprint, her busy life will become unwieldy and difficult to manage. Success and failure can be all encompassing and the energy required to survive and thrive can leave nothing in the tank for the other parts of her Life Blueprint.

As Regina's entrepreneurial business expands, chaos management can easily arrive. Imagination can begin to outrun attention to detail. New employees seldom have details of their responsibility, accountability, and authority documented. They are not kept in the loop from a macro perspective. This empowers few employees to think on their own.

With a dictatorial entrepreneur boss, mistakes crop up because Relaxation and Enjoyment are usually low. All within the company look to the "boss" for all the answers. This will stifle growth and multiple locations could be disastrous. Regina knows this.

Preparing for her second restaurant and potentially her third, fourth and more, she is busy documenting all of the procedures for opening and closing her shop, as well as the methods of cooking the food with the highest quality of ingredients and McDonald's-type precision.

Regina is busy training her key employees in order for them to advance within her Blueprint and its well-defined Vision and Big Rocks.

Will she ultimately prevail? Yes. I expect her to succeed.

There are more than **twenty-eight million small businesses** in the U.S. and over twenty-two million Americans are self-employed, with no additional payroll or employees according to the Small Business Administration. Here are some more facts from the SBA:

- ▶ Small businesses account for fifty-four percent of all U.S. sales.
- ▶ They provide fifty-five percent of all jobs and all net new jobs since the 1970s.
- ▶ The 600,000 plus franchised small businesses in the U.S. account for forty percent of all retail sales and provide jobs for some eight million people.

▶ The small business sector in America occupies thirty to fifty percent of all commercial space, an estimated twenty to thirty-four billion square feet.

While corporate America has been "downsizing," the rate of entrepreneurial "start-ups" has grown, and the rate for small business failures has declined.

◆ The number of small businesses in the U.S. has increased forty-nine percent since 1982.
◆ Since 1990, as big business eliminated four million jobs, small businesses added eight million new jobs.

Small business is obviously big business.

Starting or owning a small business in today's economy is still risky. It takes courage, cash, consistency and commitment. Experience definitely helps. Without The Blueprint, your chance of survival will be greatly diminished.

According to the U.S. Bureau of Labor Statistics, "About half of all new establishments survive five years or more and about one-third survive ten years or more. The probability of survival increases with a firm's age."

You are the ultimate boss of your entrepreneurial enterprise. Keep your eye on the ball. You are in charge of everything from marketing to opening and closing your doors. Do you see the Big Picture and do you share it with your team? You're the boss and the visionary!

The following story represents the champion mindset required of a single person entity (as in freelance graphic design or blogger) seeking to evolve into a successful entrepreneur enterprise with multiple employees:

It was already a hot day as three men boarded a bus together in the early morning hours. They were being transported to a construction site to begin their eight hours of arduous labor.

Each man had the same job. All made the same wage.

After several hours in the cruel sun, the men took a short break under the shade of a nearby tree. A passerby asked the first man what he did for a living. The disgruntled laborer scowled and replied, "I put one brick on top of another. Then I do it again."

The passerby then asked the second man the same question. He answered with no feeling, "I do construction for a living."

The third man was smiling, whistling and looking cheerful. The passerby said, "Why are you so happy? Aren't you a laborer like your friends?" The third man laughed and said, "I'm happy because I'm building a beautiful church where the congregation can go and thank God for their blessings. I'm blessed to be a part of that."

Three men. Each paid the same wage. Each had the same job. But only one knew that he was an integral part of something greater than himself.

If you are an entrepreneurial owner or small business employer, share the dream from the top to the bottom of your team. Share your Vision. Sell the holistic purpose of each part. Let everyone know that each part of the job is essential.

Know the big picture in what you do. Let the big picture inspire you as you chip away at the parts of your small business.

Three men boarded a bus taking them home from the work site. The first man got off the bus and went straight to the local bar. There he sat and complained about life before going home. The second man was grumpy as he stepped from the bus. He went home and told his wife how hard he worked for so little.

The third man was the last one to leave the bus. He collected himself and put on a big smile before he entered his front door. There he used the 90-Second Rule™ as he greeted each family members. His family always greets him at the door. He is blessed.

Which person's mindset do you foster in your business? Get everyone in the Zone knowing that you and every team member are an integral part of something greater than yourself. Smile as you work the parts of everything you do. Pass the smile forward. Know that you and all employees matter! Make your company relevant in the marketplace. Act like it from top to bottom.

Your Entrepreneur Blueprint

> The following Visions, Big Rocks, Tasks, and Key People have been placed on The Blueprint from hundreds of small business owners and entrepreneurs. These men and women are the backbone of our economy. Place strategic timelines for each of the following and incorporate them within your overall business calendar.

Possible Entrepreneur Visions *(add, edit, or delete as you see fit)*: $XYZ gross sales; $XYZ net profit; develop business processes; build the best team possible; capture twenty-five percent of local market share; expand territory; leverage product line; franchise.

Possible Entrepreneur Big Rocks *(add, edit, or delete as you see fit)*: Acquire and train business inner circle; hire new COO; build board of directors; join Young Presidents' Organization (YPO); train sales team; hire ZoneCoach® as business coach; redesign website; use re-targeting; redesign promotional material; hire PR company; cut workforce fifteen percent; purchase office building; add new product.

Possible Entrepreneur Tasks *(add, edit, or delete as you see fit)*: Write letter to board member prospects; procure asphalt paving estimates; retain realtor; walk-thru property; fire comptroller; interview web design team; read *The Blueprint*; update LinkedIn; photograph new product line; write weekly blog; write-up opening/ closing procedures; and so forth.

Possible Entrepreneur Key People *(add, edit, or delete as you see fit)*: Leadership team; COO; vice president; HR outsource personnel; CPA; executive coach; ZoneCoach®; banker; financial planner; insurance agent; business advisors; attorney; realtor; key vendor; bookkeeper; CEO; CFO; sales manager; administrative assistant; chief of staff; office manager; advertising agency contact; parents; social media expert; golf professional; sibling; son; daughter; spouse; and so on.

These Key People can have influence over your retirement; financial independence; savings accounts; net worth; business valuation; business expansion; negative stress; anxiety; worry; fear; overall happiness; and so on.

Rate your Entrepreneur S.C.O.R.E.® Level:
(1 to 10 with 10 being high)

S.	C.	O.	R.	E.
__	__	__	__	__

PART 5

Your Sports Blueprint

This section contains sports specific information garnered from personally coaching ten professional sports and every amateur sport, including swimming, track and field, skiing, volleyball, lacrosse, diving, curling, poker, ice dancing, bowling, billiards, and many more.

CHAPTER 31

Your Sports Arena

Professional and amateur athletes will share this Life Arena. Some will choose this Arena as a hobby, weekend experience, serious competitive activity, or a springboard to a professional career. A multi-sport high school athlete will choose Sports as a major Arena while selecting baseball, football, and soccer as his sub-Arenas.

The Sports Arena is highly competitive. It will require high levels of Self-discipline, Concentration, Optimism, Relaxation, and Enjoyment for you to compete. The need to attract the Zone in this Arena will be commonplace for you, your team members, and competitors.

Over forty years ago, I walked onto the tennis court to play my childhood idol, former world #1 professional **Pancho Gonzalez**. After my humbling defeat, Pancho said to me in the locker room after the match, "Son, you're good but you need more experience." I was definitely bummed.

What is experience? Is it quantity of time with a specific subject or is it quality? Or is it both? After nearly four decades, I've determined it is quality that counts the most. This is why someone young can climb to the top, while the so-called experienced performer sits on the sideline and watches the youthful ascend.

What is experience? It is a collection of four distinct time elements of a performance. This is one unit of experience.

They are:

1. **Pre-performance time**: This is the amount of time, from a few seconds to years before a specific event, of executing tasks, techniques, or routines in your sport. It is here that visions, goals, strategies, tactics, and time management are prepared or not prepared.

   The champion athlete is always the best prepared.

2. **Performance time**: This is the amount of time from the start and finish of any performance. Here you can adjust or not adjust to changing conditions, circumstances, or situations.

   Champions swiftly adjust. Non-champions wait too long to adjust or don't adjust at all, and this typically finds them lost during intense "moments of truth."

3. **Post-performance time**: This is the seconds, minutes, hours, or days after a performance where analysis and evaluation does or does not take place. This is where learning resides.

   Champions treat winning and losing the same. They are non-emotional in evaluating during post-performance time. They learn from what transpired.

   Non-champions get giddy when they win and get bummed out when they lose. They react with emotion as they blame others, offer excuses, judge everyone else, and feel like a victim of the condition, circumstance, or situation. They don't learn.

4. **Re-tool time**: This is the time to apply what you learned. Decide whether to prepare the same or change your approach to your next performance.

   Champions learn and move on. Non-champions have no clue.

These four periods of time contribute to your positive or negative experience. Each unit of experience blends into the next to form a delicate chain that becomes your sport career.

Champions prepare, adjust, evaluate, and re-tool all their performances.

All athlete performers possess the same amount of time. How you manage these four time segments determines the quality of your experience. If you do not prepare, adjust, evaluate, and re-tool properly, it may take you twice as long or more to accomplish your best. The quality of time, therefore, is the master ingredient of successful achievement. This is how...

▶ An inspired novice can gain ground on the grizzled, seasoned veteran.

▶ An inexperienced team in quantity of performances takes on the giants of sport.

▶ A highly motivated foreign athlete moves to America and in a short amount of time leapfrogs the homeland competition.

▶ An older performer can withstand the surging onslaught of the inexperienced.

▶ A new successful sports career triumphs without fear or trepidation.
▶ The young overtake the old.
▶ You can jumpstart a stagnant season or career.
▶ You can swiftly re-invent yourself and your game.

Which part of your experiences is the weakest link? Do you prepare your best? Do you adjust with a champion's decisiveness? Do you analyze and evaluate with objectivity, free from emotional judgment? Do you learn swiftly in order to prepare better for the next time? What is the quality of the units of experience in your sport?

Be forewarned to eliminate the possibility that your "I'm more experienced" mindset loses out to a champion performer that gets it. Take heed before the rookie overtakes you in your sport. Pay attention to your worn-out ways of playing your game. Learn and re-tool from your strategic and tactical miscalculations. Consistently prepare, adjust, evaluate, and re-tool your performances. Enhance the quality of time for playing golf, tennis, or another sport.

Every performance is impacted by the four levels of experience.

Great athletes are reducing their quantity of time spent in chasing their dreams. They are beating the competition in this highly competitive environment with this "less quantity but higher quality" mentality.

Take charge of your sports future now! Add quality to your units of experience and you will gain traction in becoming your genuine, authentic best athlete.

Caution: Due to the high intensity of this Arena, avoid dragging the remnants of your performances into your other Life Arenas. When your sports performance is over, it's over! "Next Arena" is your only thought.

Your Sports Blueprint

The following Visions, Big Rocks, Tasks, and Key People have been selected from the hundreds of successful amateur and professional athletes I have coached. Place strategic timelines for each of the following and incorporate them within your overall sports calendar.

Possible Sports Visions *(add, edit, or delete as you see fit)*: Personal sports records; world champion; conference champion; club champion; best athlete possible; All-Star; All-Pro; #1 ranking; Top 10 ranking; PGA, LPGA, or Champions Tour status; All-American; college scholarship; league champion; high school varsity starter; All-Conference; All-State; Mid-Am Champion; state champion; NFL player; World Cup player; club champion; tournament winner.

Possible Sports Big Rocks *(add, edit, or delete as you see fit)*: A .350 batting average; 2.9 ERA; 200 bowling average; personal record time; serve percentage; passer rating; Greens in Regulation; 40-yard dash speed; consistent starts; make swift adjustments; learn S.C.O.R.E.® System; be physically fit; gain fifteen pounds; optimum body weight; retain fitness guru; hire ZoneCoach®; and so on.

Possible Sports Tasks *(add, edit, or delete as you see fit)*: Memorize, practice, and use Universal 13™ Tools; visualize converting spares; visualize making 10-foot or less putts; visualize executing football receiver routes; create and adhere to pre-performance routines; evaluate consistently without emotion; watch film of last performance; run ten, 40-yard sprints 3x weekly; weight lift 3x weekly; make 100, four-foot putts in a row; play ZoneCoach® "Moment of Truth Game"; shoot 500 balls daily; hit fifty serves daily in ad court.

Possible Sports Key People *(add, edit, or delete as you see fit)*: coach; manager; assistant coaches; trainer; massage therapist; statistician; team captains; teammates; doubles partner; consultant; archrival; instructor; sports psychologist; ZoneCoach®; and so on.

These *Sports Key People* can have influence over your potential realization; pre-performance preparation; ability to adjust during a performance; post-performance evaluation; overall performance; S.C.O.R.E.® Level; discipline; confidence; worry; anxiety; fear; and so forth.

Rate your Sports S.C.O.R.E.® Level:
(1 to 10 with 10 being high)

S.	C.	O.	R.	E.
—	—	—	—	—

CHAPTER 32

Specific Sports Arenas

This chapter discusses potential sport specific Visions, Big Rocks, Tasks, and Key People. Regardless of your sport, the mental aspects of performance will elevate you from good to great. Managing your S.C.O.R.E.® Level will be vital for your sports success.

Each of the following sport's Visions, Big Rocks, Tasks, and Key People are from my past and current clients.

Your Golf Arena

It was a Saturday morning and the University of Illinois men's golf team arrived at my home. Culminating a long road trip, Illinois Coach **Mike Small** and his squad stopped in to listen and learn about playing golf in the Zone. They were ranked in the NCAA top-10 and they were hungry for more.

Each player was asked which S.C.O.R.E.® element they would select if he arrived at a drive-up window where Self-discipline, Concentration, Optimism, Relaxation, and Enjoyment could be ordered. Some players chose a slab of discipline, bucket of focus, basket of confidence, and bag of relaxation. Each player possessed heightened awareness of what they needed in order for the Zone to arrive.

"Jim Fannin's S.C.O.R.E.® System has given our team an edge. It's been instrumental in our program's success," echoes Coach Small. "Each team member understands they are more than golfers and this balance has kept us away from the roller-coaster highs and lows of competitive golf."

This group of young men knew what they wanted from their college experience. All envisioned playing on the PGA Tour. All perceived a National Championship and each knew what he needed to help his team get there. Each had The Blueprint for winning golf and more importantly for being a great student, son, brother, friend, significant other, and lastly, their genuine, authentic, best self.

233

The University of Illinois Men's Golf Team has been one of the best in the nation for a decade. **Mike Small**, their coach and the NCAA Coach of the Year, has created an atmosphere of peak performance and overall success. Two individual national champions were developed and eight Big 10 titles (and counting) have been garnered. They are Zone performers!

What a great game! The mission of golf is to place a white ball into eighteen cups with the least amount of strokes. A golf course designer adds water, sand, trees, and undulating greens as obstacles for the golfer to achieve his or her mission. Oh yes...they spread the holes out over a 6,000- to 7,000-yard obstacle course. This test of discipline, focus, confidence, relaxation, strategy, tactics and skill takes approximately five hours. This creates an epic concentration challenge. Mental and physical endurance are required.

This Sports Arena is tough. The difference in winning and losing is a few strokes. Mistake tolerance is required to be successful. Present tense thinking is a must. Avoiding the past during your round is mandatory. Going into the future is brief and it's to choose your target, club, and shape of your shot.

Once you leave the course or range, close the door on golf and refocus on the other aspects of life. Likewise, once you leave the other aspects of life, have the mantra, "There's no place I'd rather be than right here, right now."

Time to play Golf in the Zone™.

Your Golf Blueprint

The following Visions, Big Rocks, Tasks, and Key People have been selected from scores of successful PGA and LPGA professionals, high school and college All-Americans, and other successful amateur and professional golfers. This Golf Blueprint™ and the S.C.O.R.E.® System have helped 10 golfers win their first professional tournament and golfers attain #1 world ranking, NCAA Champion, Big 10 titles, Ryder Cup, Walker Cup & Curtis Cup teams, LPGA Major, and scores of private and public championships. Place strategic timelines for each of the following and incorporate these within your overall golf calendar.

Possible Golf Visions *(add, edit, or delete as you see fit)*: World's #1 ranking; world's top 10 ranking; PGA or LPGA Tour; Masters Champion; Ryder Cup Team; Walker Cup Team; scratch golf; specific handicap; scoring average; rounds per year; golf travel; club champion; conference champion; college scholarship; All-American; amateur championships; All-State; league champion.

Possible Golf Big Rocks *(add, edit, or delete as you see fit)*: Golf travel; Masters attendance; play Pebble Beach; master S.C.O.R.E.® System; sixty-five percent fairways; sixty percent Greens in Regulation; twenty-nine putts per round; average twelve birdie opportunities within twenty-five feet per round; hire top golf instructor; break personal sand save percentage; purchase new golf clubs; hire ZoneCoach®; Attend Golf in the Zone™ School; play bogie-free round.

Possible Golf Tasks *(add, edit, or delete as you see fit)*: In practice, stroke 100 putts in a row from four feet; play a practice round with no technical thoughts; practice the 90-Second Rule™ after each hole; create your standard, competitive round evaluation; utilize Russian Dolls™ visualization; memorize, practice, and use Universal 13™ Tools; visualize hitting every club in your bag accurately; play 100 practice holes this week.

235

Possible Golf Key People *(add, edit, or delete as you see fit)*: Swing coach; putting guru; physical trainer; ZoneCoach®; playing partner; massage therapist; sports psychologist; physician; club fitter; nutritionist; club manufacturer; sports agent; sponsors; college coach; high school coach; wife; parents; sibling; golf director; teammates; and so on.

These Golf Key People can have influence over your potential realization; pre-round preparation; ability to adjust during a round; post-round evaluation; overall performance; technical proficiency; physical fitness; S.C.O.R.E.® Level; discipline; confidence; worry; anxiety; fear; etc.

Rate your Golf S.C.O.R.E.® Level:
(1 to 10 with 10 being high)

S.	C.	O.	R.	E.
___	___	___	___	___

Your Tennis Arena

As a former international player and coach, tennis launched my current coaching career and it spawned the ZoneCoach® in me.

The Tennis Arena is for junior or adult amateur players, junior high, high school or college players, aspiring professionals, or career professionals on the Association of ATP or Women's Tennis Association Tours.

Tennis (unlike most golf events) is a psychological combat sport where you can see and feel the competitive presence of your opponent. You are mentally, physically, or technically prepared to adjust your performance or not. This Arena requires you to move and think in short spurts for over an hour or longer. Because of intense competition, your mind needs a combination of clarity, decisiveness, relaxation, and relentless focus.

Tennis is the only game that allows great comebacks, due to no time clock. In fact, if you are losing to your opponent with a score of 0-6; 0-5 in a two-set match, the next game begins with a 0-0 score. You still have a chance (albeit slim) to win. This fact turns tennis into a physical, technical, and mental chess match that can last hours.

The primary goal in tennis is to win each point by hitting the ball over the net one more time than your opponent. To accomplish this a successful player requires high levels of **S**elf-discipline, **C**oncentration, **O**ptimism, **R**elaxation, and **E**njoyment. Managing your personal S.C.O.R.E.® Level provides the greatest opportunity for tennis victories.

In the 1980s and 1990s, my S.C.O.R.E.® Tennis Academy in Countryside, Illinois, (with partner Peter Fleming) housed the world's largest private tennis academy. We developed champions. International, national, and state champion amateurs, the #1 professional from 16 different countries (all played on ATP or WTA Tours) visited our indoor facility seeking advice, change, and of course...The Blueprint.

Every one of our dozen coaches was an integral part of his or her student's master plan. With The Tennis Blueprint™ we prescribed the details and timeline needed for improvement in order to manifest the overarching vision.

Over $24 million in college scholarships has been garnered with The Blueprint.

Chronologically mapping when to peak mentally, physically, and technically is an art form and it's crucial for continued progress and overall success. Both amateurs and professionals took this very seriously. This makes The Blueprint mandatory.

In creating The Tennis Blueprint™ you need to know exactly what you want to accomplish and when it will happen. With this knowledge, you can now work on the mental, physical, and technical aspects of your game that will carry you to victory.

Every professional tennis player I coached had a well-defined Blueprint. The agreed upon manuscript dictated the tournament schedule, practice agenda, as well as the time away from the game.

For most of my tennis clients, physically and mentally peaking during a major tournament was the quest. This required working chronologically backwards (B2A Principle™). If we needed to hone a specific stroke or shot, we found the time in the off-season or when we had at least two weeks between tournaments. Otherwise, we worked on our strengths as a tournament approached.

With my world top-fifty ranked clients, we spent time working on all phases of the game. However, an inordinate amount of time was on the mental side. Every match was charted from a mental perspective and these are a few items that were incorporated into The Blueprint.

- Since most service breaks of one client occurred after change-overs, we designed mental routines during this 90-second break in the action to reverse this statistic.

- Once I realized that the player that reached 30 (30-0; 30-15) in the majority of the games, won the match 100 percent of the time, we practiced sets where reaching 30 first automatically won the game. Practicing this became a game changer. Obviously, in theory you can be down love-30 every game and still win the match. With over 1,000 matches charted, however, this never happened.

- Winning three points in a row over two games initiated or continued the momentum of the match. This awareness helped several players make positive energy runs.

- Three unforced errors in a row were NOT acceptable. Players continued to hit out on all shots but their targets became more conservative and less risky. Stop the bleeding was the awareness.

- We replaced the term "holding serve" with "taking serve." This mindset shift produced fewer breaks and more clutch serves, especially when serving up a break.

Obviously, we created goals for improving groundstrokes, return of serve, serve percentage and effectiveness, approach shots, volleys, serve and volley, overheads, lobs and overall defense. However, we spent an inordinate amount of time on the mental side of the game.

With The Tennis Blueprint™ tucked securely under The Blueprint, my clients and I were and are always on the same page. We measured our Blueprint progress against match results and we adjusted swiftly, if needed.

Every amateur and professional tennis champion I've coached had a Tennis Blueprint™.

Your Tennis Blueprint

The following Visions, Big Rocks, Tasks, and Key People have been placed on The Tennis Blueprint™ of thousands of junior and adult amateurs, ranging from seven national champions, dozens of state champions and hundreds of ranked players to the #1 professional from 16 countries and seven players in the world's top-10, including a French Open Champion and runner-up and a four-time Wimbledon champion, as well as the Italian Davis Cup team. Place strategic timelines for each of the following and incorporate them within your overall tennis calendar.

Possible Tennis Visions *(add, edit, or delete as you see fit)***:** World's #1; World's Top 10; ATP or WTA Tour; Wimbledon Champion; club champion; conference champion; college scholarship; All-American; bolster USTA ranking to next level; amateur championships; All-State; league champion; national championship; national top 10 ranking; national ranking; district ranking; regional ranking.

Possible Tennis Big Rocks *(add, edit, or delete as you see fit)***:** Tennis travel; Wimbledon or U.S. Open attendance; sixty-five percent average serve percentage; ten or less unforced errors per set; visit top tennis pro; improve overhead; own ad court wide serve; learn backhand topspin lob; purchase new rackets; hire ZoneCoach®; increase endurance (run one mile in under six minutes).

Possible Tennis Tasks *(add, edit, or delete as you see fit)***:** Hit fifty groundstrokes in a row in practice; hit 100 serves in practice; play a practice set with no technical thoughts; practice the 90-Second Rule™ after each game; create your standard, competitive round evaluation; play left-handed players in practice; play steady baseliner in practice; utilize Russian Dolls™; memorize, practice and use Universal 13™ Tools; visualize hitting every shot with accuracy; run ten, 40-yard dashes all under 4.8 seconds; run five miles daily (collectively under 30 minutes).

Possible Tennis Key People *(add, edit, or delete as you see fit)*: Tennis professional; physical trainer; ZoneCoach®; doubles partner; hitting partner(s); physician; massage therapist; sports psychologist; racket stringer; nutritionist; racket manufacturer representative; sports agent; sponsors; college coach; high school coach; parents; wife; sibling; tennis director; teammates; and so on.

These Tennis Key People can have influence over your potential realization; pre-match preparation; ability to adjust during a match; post-match evaluation; overall performance; S.C.O.R.E.® Level; physical fitness; technical proficiency; discipline; patience; confidence; worry; anxiety; fear; and so forth.

Rate your Tennis S.C.O.R.E.® Level:
(1 to 10 with 10 being high)

S.	C.	O.	R.	E.
—	—	—	—	—

Your Baseball (Softball) Arena

Joey Cora was a lifetime .267 switch-hitting second baseman for the Chicago White Sox when I met him. He was not an everyday starter. He was traded to the Seattle Mariners as an afterthought add-on and was soon relegated to the Pacific Northwest. Before the next season, Joey and I discussed what he wanted. He envisioned hitting an overall .300 batting average, making the All-Star team, hitting home runs right-handed (which he had never done even in Little League or other organized play), and signing a multi-million dollar contract.

Of all my clients, Joey Cora was by far the most disciplined.

Cora's biggest challenge was to be the starting second baseman because his goals could only be reached as a starter. This visualization took place dozens of times daily over the off-season and the time had now arrived.

As Cora prepared for the game, he watched his manager, **Lou Piniella,** post the starting line-up on the wall and Joey's name was absent. He immediately shut his eyes and envisioned his name on the roster. Within seconds, Piniella came back to the roster and scratched out his starting second baseman and wrote Cora into the line-up.

Why did Lou do this? Since I was working with Piniella I asked him. He said, "I just had a gut feeling." And we know that gut feeling arrived intuitively from Joey Cora's Zone mindset.

Cora went on to make the All-Star team, hit .300 for the year and sign a big contract. And YES he hit multiple home runs right-handed that year.

Joey Cora had a Baseball Blueprint™

Baseball is a team game, but the key to a player's success is dictated by his or her ability to prepare, adjust, and evaluate objectively. Joey Cora mastered this and is now coaching in the MLB.

The Baseball Arena is for male or female junior or adult amateur players, junior high, high school or college players, aspiring professionals, or career professionals.

This Arena has pitching, hitting, and fielding as its major performance parts. The following is the essence of the craft and this has been delivered personally to ALL baseball clients:

- ▶ Pitchers throw baseballs or softballs to well-defined targets with late-breaking stuff.
- ▶ Hitters stroke baseballs or softballs solid with an accelerated bat head.
- ▶ Fielders give themselves more time (to get to the ball) in order to give the offense less time to get to the base.

The Visions, Big Rocks, Tasks, and Key People have jurisdiction over the above three parts of the game.

Your Baseball Blueprint

The following Visions, Big Rocks, Tasks, and Key People have been extracted from The Blueprint of twenty-six MLB All-Stars, five MVPs, four Cy Young Award winners, Gold Glove and Silver Slugger recipients from every position, two HR champs and two Hall of Famers, as well as high school and college All-Americans and many other notable successes, such as **Mike Cameron, Carlos Delgado**, and **J.D. Martinez** smacking four HRs in one game. Place strategic timelines for each of the following and incorporate them within your overall baseball calendar.

Possible Baseball Visions *(add, edit, or delete as you see fit)*: World Series' MVP; Triple Crown winner; MLB contract; batting title; All-Star; .300 batting average; .350 batting average; .400 batting average; 2.9 ERA; Hall of Fame; high school or college varsity starter; high school or college All-Conference selection; high school or college All-American; MLB first round draft choice; Gold Glove recipient; Cy Young award winner; Silver Slugger award; college scholarship.

Possible Baseball Big Rocks *(add, edit, or delete as you see fit)*: World Series attendance; visit Cooperstown; maximize mental game; daily visualize all pitches; dry swing all nine hitting zones; master breathing six to eight breaths per minute; create pre-hitting routines; ten or fewer errors annually; hire hitting or pitching guru; attend summer camp; star in Cape Cod or other summer league; increase velocity; command three pitches; develop change-up; dominate inside pitches; maintain poise during adversity; increase concentration.

Possible Baseball Tasks *(add, edit, or delete as you see fit)*: Hit eight solid balls in a row during batting practice; visualize hitting solid; pitch with no technical thoughts; practice the 90-Second Rule™ after each at bat; utilize Russian Dolls™ visualization; memorize, practice, and use Universal 13™ Tools; create your standard, competitive game evaluation;

visualize hitting solid with power; run ten, 40-yard dashes all under 4.8 seconds; acquire new bats; research, interview, and hire ZoneCoach®; run five miles daily (under thirty minutes).

Possible Baseball Key People *(add, edit, or delete as you see fit)*: Hitting or pitching guru; physical trainer; ZoneCoach®; catcher; hitting partner(s); physician; massage therapist; sports psychologist; nutritionist; equipment manufacturer representative; baseball agent; sponsors; college coach; high school coach; summer league coaches; wife; parents; siblings; teammates; and so on.

These Baseball (Softball) Key People can have influence over your potential realization; pre-game preparation; ability to adjust during a game; post-game evaluation; overall performance; S.C.O.R.E.® Level; physical fitness; technical proficiency (hitting, base running, fielding, pitching); discipline; patience; confidence; worry; anxiety; fear; and so on.

Rate your Baseball S.C.O.R.E.® Level:
(1 to 10 with 10 being high)

S.　　C.　　O.　　R.　　E.

___　 ___　 ___　 ___　 ___

Your Basketball Arena

He was the 1994 ACC Player of the Year, a two-time NCAA All-American, and a two-time NCAA champion. As a professional, he was the 1995 NBA co-Rookie of the Year, a seven-time NBA All-Star, and a five-time All NBA selection.

Why would **Grant Hill** need coaching from the ZoneCoach®? Quickly, I knew that he was a man who did everything in his power to be the best he could be. He left no stone unturned. Excellence was his quest. Taking his mind to a consistent Zone standard was his goal.

Grant also knew he was more than a basketball player. His family didn't take a backseat to his profession. He was and still is a true champion in every respect.

Loy Vaught played power forward for the LA Clippers. This night however, would be different. With injuries to his starting center, Loy would have to play out of position and face the great Hall of Fame center, **Hakeem Olajuwon**, of the Houston Rockets. On the phone with me, Loy envisioned taking his one-on-one competitor ten to fifteen feet from the basket where he would drive the rim or drain his patented short-range jumper. That night belonged to Loy Vaught. As a Zone performer, he out-scored and out-rebounded Olajuwon with a masterful Zone performance that had me screaming at the TV set with encouragement and celebration.

The **Basketball Arena** is for male or female junior or adult amateur players, junior high, high school or college players, aspiring professionals or career professionals.

This Arena has shooting, ball handling, and rebounding as its major performance parts.

- **Shooters** shoot basketballs to well-defined targets.
- **Ball handlers** give themselves more time in order to give the defense less time to defend the passing lanes or shots.
- **Rebounders** give themselves more time (watching the ball off the glass) in order to give the offense or defense less time to get to the ball.

The Visions, Big Rocks, Tasks, and Key People have jurisdiction over the above three parts of the game.

Your Basketball Blueprint

The following Visions, Big Rocks, Tasks, and Key People have been taken from NBA and WNBA players and scores of All-Americans from high school and college. Place strategic timelines for each of the following and incorporate these within your overall basketball calendar.

Possible Basketball Visions *(add, edit, or delete as you see fit)*: NBA Finals MVP; NBA All-Star; NBA contract; WNBA contract; scoring title; Hall of Fame; high school or college varsity starter; high school and/or college All-Conference selection; All-State; All-American; NCAA Final Four; NCAA champion; college scholarship.

Possible Basketball Big Rocks *(add, edit, or delete as you see fit)*: NCAA Final Four attendance; attend prominent basketball camp; hire private shooting coach; hire private ball handling coach; master S.C.O.R.E.® System; .50 percent Field Goal Percentage; forty percent 3-Point shooting percentage; ten rebounds per game average; fifteen PPG (points per game) average; twenty PPG average; master breathing technique of six to eight breaths per minute; create pre-game routines; attend basketball summer camp; star in AAU or other summer league; increase endurance.

Possible Basketball Tasks *(add, edit, or delete as you see fit)*: Make four, 3-point shots in a row from different positions; shoot 500 balls daily (summer); dribble daily; dribble with the opposite hand every day for a week; visualize bank shots from both sides of basket; play with zero negative thoughts; practice mental intensity while staying physically relaxed; utilize Russian Dolls™; memorize, practice, and use Universal 13™ Tools; create standard, competitive game evaluation; visualize driving with the opposite hand to the hole; run ten, 40-yard dashes all under 4.8 seconds; meditate daily; interview and hire ZoneCoach®; run five miles daily (under thirty minutes).

248

Possible Basketball Key People *(add, edit, or delete as you see fit)*: Shooting or ball-handling guru; physical trainer; massage therapist; nutritionist; physician; ZoneCoach®; practice partner; manufacturer representative; sports psychologist; basketball agent; sponsors; college coach; high school coach; summer league coaches; parents; wife; siblings; teammates; and so forth.

These Basketball Key People can have influence over your potential realization; pre-game preparation; ability to adjust during a game; post-game evaluation; overall performance; S.C.O.R.E.® Level; physical fitness; technical proficiency; discipline; patience; confidence; worry; anxiety; fear; and so on.

Rate your Basketball S.C.O.R.E.® Level:
(1 to 10 with 10 being high)

S.	C.	O.	R.	E.
___	___	___	___	___

Your Football Arena

Alex Ramart is a freshman quarterback on scholarship at the University of Akron. He is the epitome of a Zone performer. He is on a mission in his quest for excellence.

He reaches his performance standards daily. He knows who he is and what he needs to do to get to the next level. Nightly, he envisions throwing to well-defined targets. He imagines situations and circumstances in various conditions in order to be the best prepared he can be. Alex is a champion.

Alex Ramart is also a great leader of men. By example, he does not shy away from hard work or adversity and he offers simple and direct encouragement openly and freely to his offense team members. But he knows he's more than a football player. Although he has placed a lot of "happy eggs" in his Football Arena, he has prepared for life after football.

Playing in the NFL is one of Alex's Visions. He knows the NFL is littered with career tragedies. Here is the nightmare. Within two years of retirement, 78 percent of NFL players are bankrupt or in severe financial turmoil, according the NFL Player's Union. Hard to believe, isn't it? How can men who earn so much have so little after retirement? Alex is prepared with plan B in The Blueprint, if and when, his possible NFL career is over.

Evan Pilgram was not a starter for the Chicago Bears and he was an afterthought for management. The first night we met he visualized starting as the Bear's offensive center.

Ironically, he was a former All-American offensive guard and had NEVER played center. My intuition recommended the visualization and Evan went with it. Within a week, the line coach moved Evan to center and a week later he started against the Vikings in Soldier Field.

Visualization works!

The Football Arena is for male junior or adult amateur players, high school or college players, aspiring professionals or career professionals.

This Arena has both offense and defensive positions. The goal of each player on either side of the ball is to give yourself more time (mentally focusing on the other side of the scrimmage line) in order to give the opposition less time to execute blocks, tackles, passes, or runs.

▸ Offensive players give themselves more time to find receivers; run between holes in the defense; and block defenders.
▸ Defensive players give themselves more time in order to give the offense less time to find passing and or running lanes, scramble out of the pocket and execute passes and running plays.

The Visions, Big Rocks, Tasks, and Key People have jurisdiction over the above two parts of the game (yes, special teams are important and they are placed within offensive or defense).

Your Football Blueprint

The following Visions, Big Rocks, Tasks, and Key People have been selected from scores of successful All-Pros, high school and college All-Americans and other successful amateur and professional football players. Place strategic timelines for each of the following and incorporate them within your overall football calendar.

Possible Football Visions *(add, edit, or delete as you see fit)***:** Super Bowl MVP; NFL All-Pro; NFL contract; rushing title; Hall of Fame; high school or college varsity starter; high school and or college All-Conference selection; All-State; All-American; college scholarship.

Possible Football Big Rocks *(add, edit, or delete as you see fit)***:** Super Bowl attendance; Super Bowl champion; attend prominent football camp; hire private quarterback coach; create nutritional plan; hire nutritionist; hire private receivers coach; master S.C.O.R.E.® System; 100 percent PAT; lead NFL passer rating; one sack per game average; hire ZoneCoach®; master breathing technique of six to eight breaths per minute; create pre-game routines; visit performance guru; bench press 300 pounds; ten percent body fat; increase endurance; run 4.6 in 40-yard dash.

Possible Football Tasks *(add, edit, or delete as you see fit)***:** Weight train 4x weekly; throw or catch 100 balls daily (summer); mentally and physically practice routes, plays, techniques, assignments, and so forth; adhere to nutritional plan; sleep eight hours nightly; play with no negative thoughts; practice mental intensity while staying physically relaxed; utilize Russian Dolls™; memorize, practice, and use Universal 13™ Tools; create your standard, competitive game evaluation; visualize "bull rush" technique; run ten, 40-yard dashes 3x weekly (all under 4.8 seconds); meditate daily; interview and hire ZoneCoach®; run five miles daily (under thirty minutes).

Possible Football Key People *(add, edit, or delete as you see fit)***:** Throwing or receiving guru; physical trainer; ZoneCoach®; nutritionist; physician; sports psychologist; strength coach; practice partner; football agent; sponsors; college scholarship consultant; college coach; high school coach; summer league coaches; parents; wife; siblings; teammates; and so forth.

These Football Key People can have influence over your potential realization; pre-game preparation; ability to adjust during a game; post-game evaluation; overall performance; S.C.O.R.E.® Level; physical fitness; technical proficiency; discipline; patience; confidence; worry; anxiety; fear; and so on.

Rate your Football S.C.O.R.E.® Level:
(1 to 10 with 10 being high)

S.	C.	O.	R.	E.
__	__	__	__	__

Your Soccer Arena

Peter Nowak worked hard to attain the MVP for the Chicago Fire. He was a master on the field. Upon retirement, he was hired as the head coach for DC United. In his maiden season, the MLS acquired the highest paid contract for it youngest player ever.... **Freddie Adu.** I attended pre-season training in Florida and the buzz about young Freddie was mounting.

At the opening game on April 3, 2004, all eyes were on Freddie. He was a child prodigy at age fourteen and the world anticipated the new Pelé. The television networks and sportswriters, with MLS approval and encouragement, set the stage for the greatest debut ever. When the game started, Freddie was on the bench and the powers that be were beside themselves. "Why is our investment NOT starting?" they pondered. Did Peter Nowak NOT get the memo about the magnitude of this opening game?"

Unbeknownst to the media and ownership, Freddie had been clobbered daily by the "older men" on DC United's team. He did NOT deserve to start even though he was getting all the headlines. Nowak asked me, "What should I do?" and I responded with "Do you want to win the MLS Cup?" "Of course," said Peter with conviction. With that I said, "Then out of respect to your team, put the best men on the field and let the chips fall where they may."

Freddie did NOT start the game in this media circus, opening day spectacle. The league officials went nuclear and at halftime, with no Freddie on the field, they stormed the locker room and I thought Nowak would immediately get fired. DC United won the game and Freddie Adu did play to a standing ovation in the second half. With team respect and solidarity, Peter Nowak led DC United to the league championship.

Soccer or football is a team game and how the team is managed dictates the performance mindset of the whole. I am now hooked on this sport and am aware of results from around the world.

The **Soccer Arena** is for male or female junior or adult amateur players, high school or college players, aspiring professionals or career professionals.

The Visions, Big Rocks, Tasks, and Key People have jurisdiction of your overall game.

Your Soccer Blueprint

The following Visions, Big Rocks, Tasks, and Key People have been extracted from The Blueprint of MLS All-Stars, MVPs, World Cup team members, high school, and college All-Americans, and many other notable successes of the game. Place strategic timelines for each of the following and incorporate them within your overall soccer calendar.

Possible Soccer Visions *(add, edit, or delete as you see fit)*: World Cup MVP; MLS contract; Manchester United contract; scoring title; All-Star; high school or college varsity starter; high school All-Conference or All-State selection; MLS First round draft choice; college scholarship; Olympic team member; World Cup champion team member.

Possible Soccer Big Rocks *(add, edit, or delete as you see fit)*: World Cup attendance; daily visualize striking accuracy; master breathing six to eight breaths per minute; hire ZoneCoach®; create pre-game routines; visit goalkeeper guru; attend summer camp; star in summer league; increase endurance; create your standard, competitive game evaluation; increase speed; excel in moving left laterally; increase footwork skills.

Possible Soccer Tasks *(add, edit, or delete as you see fit)*: Kick eight solid balls into target in a row during practice; visualize one-on-one penalty kick; play with no technical thoughts; remain positive throughout the game; utilize Russian Dolls™ visualization; memorize, practice, and use Universal 13™ Tools; adhere to pre-game and post-game routines (includes evaluation); practice footwork drills; visualize defending best player on upcoming opposition; run ten, 40-yard dashes all under 4.8 seconds; purchase or acquire new shoes; run five miles daily (under thirty minutes); interview and hire ZoneCoach®.

Possible Soccer Key People *(add, edit, or delete as you see fit)*: Goalkeeping guru; physical trainer; ZoneCoach®; speed coach; massage therapist; physician; sports psychologist; nutritionist; soccer agent; sponsors; college coach; high school coach; summer league coaches; parents; wife; siblings; teammates; and so on.

These Soccer Key People can have influence over your potential realization; pre-game preparation; ability to adjust during a game; post-game evaluation; overall performance; S.C.O.R.E.® Level; physical fitness; technical proficiency; discipline; patience; confidence; worry; anxiety; fear; and so forth.

Rate your Soccer S.C.O.R.E.® Level:
(1 to 10 with 10 being high)

S.	C.	O.	R.	E.
___	___	___	___	___

PART 6

Maintain the Life You Deserve

This section addresses the fact that getting to your best place in life is one challenge, but staying there for the rest of your life is another.

CHAPTER 33

Back to the Future

The following is being conducted by hundreds of thousands of Zoniacs™ around the globe.

Once a week, sequester yourself in a private place. Choose Friday, Saturday, or Sunday as your Vision Day and Thought Management Day. Relax. Clear your mind. Go to Higher Ground and peruse each Life Arena. Visualize each stand-alone sphere of interest with its Vision, Big Rocks, Tasks, and Key People. In addition, mentally picture each Arena with its unique conditions, circumstances, and situations.

Modify your Arenas if necessary.

See each Arena as if it's a reality TV show. Even though they are all playing simultaneously, take one at a time. Picture the coach and or co-coach interacting with the Arena's multiple Players (participants). Watch the communication dynamic on the screen of space in your mind.

Visualize your life movie.

As you mentally move from one Arena to another, see the S.C.O.R.E.® Makers and Breakers. After ascertaining your current status for each Arena, then review each again to visualize ONLY what you want.

Next...see what Big Rocks you will accomplish for your upcoming week. See each of them in completed, finished state.

Nightly, go to Higher Ground with your Primary Arena. See this Vision repetitively.

CHAPTER 34

No Bad Days…None!

Having a life with zero "bad days" is a choice. Eliminating these days will clear the way for The Blueprint to swiftly manifest.

Obviously negative things happen to good people. We can have personal loss with a loved one's surprising death. This has happened to me on five occasions. It is not pleasant.

My first major life challenge was the death of my best friend, **Brian Judd.** He was the brother of **Naomi Judd,** the Grammy Award-winning mom in the mother/daughter duo **The Judds.**

Brian and I did everything together. We played and watched sports, walked in the woods, talked about girls, played practical jokes, and laughed every day. He was the funniest person I've ever known. He always cracked me up.

One day, Brian was walking with me as I delivered newspapers door-to-door. After twenty minutes, he began complaining of a swollen node under his arm. Ironically, I had a similar lump under my arm. We both became concerned and told our parents.

After doctors' visits we received the biopsy news. Brian was diagnosed with Hodgkin's lymphoma (also known as Hodgkin's disease), a type of cancer that develops from cells in the lymphatic system (part of the body's immune system) called lymphocytes. Lymphocytes are a type of white blood cell that helps the body fight infections.

Although my tests came back negative, Brian's results devastated me.

Brian's cancer began to ravage his body. From chemotherapy, his hair fell out. He lost considerable weight. He looked sick. Even though his diagnosis was critical, his mood and overall mindset remained upbeat. He would go to the end of his life as upbeat and positive as any person could be. He was not a victim or judge. I never heard him complain.

Brian Judd was a champion. He was my hero.

The day he died was the worst day of my life. I was physically sick. I couldn't eat. It all seemed surreal. Somehow, I felt Brian reach out to me. "Never have a bad day again." Was this eerily delivered message real or my imagination? At that moment, I knew how I physically and emotionally felt, was a choice. Yes, I was extremely sad. Yes, I cried uncontrollably. However, this thought that instantly popped into my mind of never having a bad day was profound and surprisingly comforting.

On **November 8, 1965**, I pledged to honor my best friend by never having a bad day again.

Over 20,000 days (over fifty years) later with the deaths of parents and grandparents, business disappointments, family woes, physical illness and injury and other maladies, no bad days have arrived. None.

It took a tragedy to set my course of extreme positivity. I hope that will not happen to you in order to make this choice. You and I both have free will. This gift is our ultimate prize possession. Please use it wisely and use it often for improving your quality of life.

The most typical bad day occurs when your Primary Arena delivers disappointment and/or displeasure. With many individuals placing their "happy eggs" in their business baskets, a negative experience can easily spill into the Spouse, Friends, Sports, and or Self Arenas. Many overall moods rise and fall on what happens in their job, vocation and career.

By segregating your Life Arenas, you can isolate thoughts and feelings. Containment of any negativity allows entering your next Arena with a fresh attitude or positive S.C.O.R.E.˚ Level. Here's how to do it.

Never have a day you haven't already lived.

Visualize the Big Rocks for your upcoming day the night before it's to happen. See them being accomplished.

During the day, prepare to enter (mentally or physically) each Life Arena with your best S.C.O.R.E.˚ Level. Conduct a swift S.C.O.R.E.˚ Check or if you're an accomplished Zoniac™ just say or think the word S.C.O.R.E.˚ before entering. Once you are mentally or physically inside an Arena, stay in the Zone. Avoid being interrupted by your cell phone. Use 90-Second Rule™ tools to adjust if necessary. Once you leave the Arena, you can swiftly evaluate if time allows. This can be accomplished in ninety seconds or less.

Champions in life, business, and sports only go into the future for Vision planning, goal-setting, and selecting strategies and tactics.

They remain in the present more than others in the Arena. These high achievers only go into the past for analysis or evaluation. Occasionally they tell stories or share experiences to make a point or to conjure up pleasurable times with friends, colleagues or family.

Know that life can deal potentially crippling blows to your ego. Sometimes, your expectations will not meet reality. It happens to all of us. Be ready if and when adversity arrives.

CHAPTER 35

"No" Is the New "Yes"

Do you want your finger smashed in the car door? NO. Do you want to lick the frost off of the ski lift pole? NO. Do you want to swim with a Great White shark? NO. Do you want to watch your parents make out? OMG! NO! Do you want a life without The Blueprint? Knowing what I know now. Absolutely NOT.

Obviously, there are many things that we can say NO to with great certainty and finality. So why is it so hard to say NO to other people? It's even more difficult to say NO to family, friends and associates.

Start adding the power of NO and it will save you countless hours of worry and concern.

▸ Would you like another drink? NO. It will save your liver.
▸ Are you coming over tonight? NO. It will save you time.
▸ Is he your boyfriend? NO. It will establish what is and what isn't.
▸ Isn't Mary a great singer? NO. She's a good singer. It will provide clarity.

The No Imposters

Avoid the following replacements for NO. These stand-ins are fakes. They are imposters. They buy time, which helps you weigh your options *(most people are catching on to you)*. These frauds only postpone the inevitable NO. You know that NO is going to come eventually. Get it over with. Say it.

Are you coming to the party? **I'm not sure.** I may be going to see my grandmother in Vermont. She's been sick. *(You know you're not going... You'll wind up blowing this off.)*

Do you want to go eat at that new Mexican place on Halsted? **Is it any good?** *(Answering with a question is usually a cover-up for NO.)*

Are you going to the Johnson's open house? **Can I let you know tomorrow?** *(That's right...maybe they'll forget by tomorrow.)*

Will you contribute $25 to the Humane Society? **I probably will, but not right now.**

(You couldn't handle the guilt, could you?)

We're all going to the Webster Grill. Are you going? **I'm going to try**. *(You know you're not going. You're going to bail out at the last minute with some lame excuse.)*

Are you coming over tonight? **Maybe.** *(How many better options do you have? That's the real question.)*

Do you think you'll be there? **Possibly.** *(Answered with a higher pitched voice, you know you'll be a no-show.)*

Will you play in the Pro-Am with me? **I might be able to make it.** *(I bet your calendar will mysteriously become booked around tee time.)*

Do not feel guilty for using the word NO. Say it now three times... NO...NO...NO. It feels good, doesn't it? There's a certain power that comes with it. You can say NO if you want. NO is final. NO sets the barriers. NO keeps you focused. NO stops the charade. NO can end the possibility of getting in trouble. NO can end an unhealthy relationship. NO can keep you sober. NO can save you money. NO can save you time. NO can be a good friend to a good friend. NO can eliminate confusion.

NO can give you power.

NO has received a bad rap. It needs a serious PR campaign. Bad press has soured most people on NO. Everyone thinks it's so negative. NO is positive. If used at the right time and place, it can lead to success.

Listen to your gut and if it whispers NO, then say NO!

"Mom, all my girlfriends are going to Amanda's slumber party. Can I go?" *Hmmm. What does my gut say?* NO.

"You should invest in Lehman Brothers' stock." NO. *How many didn't listen to their intuition?*

"Do you want me to set you up with one of Bernie Madoff's invest-ments?" NO. *Thank goodness I listened to my inner voice.*

Yes...yes...yes...I am an eternal optimist. I am extremely positive. I talk positively in everything I do. My blood type is positive. Positive belief and expectancy are my best friends. And I know most reading this are of the same cloth. However, sprinkling in a few "No's" with your family, friends and associates will set you free. Communication will never be better.

Do you want to rent *The Legend of Hercules* starring The Rock? NO. Didn't that feel awesome?

NO is the "new" yes!

The power of "NO" will help manifest The Blueprint, turning your plan into reality. And being decisive with "NO" will give your success a resounding YES!

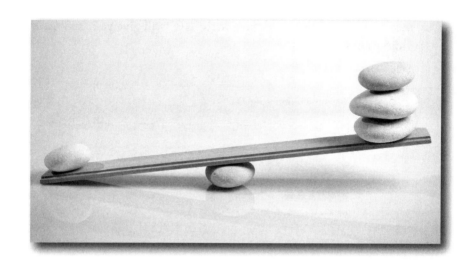

CHAPTER 36

The Teeter-Totter Effect™

THE TEETER-TOTTER EFFECT™

It is time to say NO to the Teeter-Totter Effect™.
His putting was amazing. Everything that he rolled, found the cup. If he could only have more opportunities, but his iron play was off. He either pulled it or pushed it and his accuracy was inconsistent and unpredictable. Fast forward one week... "My iron play has come around," he gloated. I'm striping it! I just wish I could buy a putt." The Teeter-Totter Effect™ has arrived.

This up and down, on again and off again performance is prevalent in life, business, and sports. Fix your marriage...struggle with parenting. Fix your finances...can't fit into your pants because you've gained an extra 15 pounds. How do you fix the inconsistencies? How do you quell the wild fluctuations in your life?

Welcome to the Teeter-Totter Effect.™

When you are focused on one thing, it's easy to forget something else. Focus on your swing and you don't focus on your stance. Focus on your forehand and you forget to pay attention to your serve. The Teeter-Totter Effect™ is normal. It happens to everyone. It is commonplace.

When you focus on one aspect of your life, golf game, or business, remind yourself to still remain positive about the items that don't have your full attention. Refuse to put them down. Don't talk about them as if they are real living things. "My swing is letting me down," I recently heard from a client. Really? You are letting you down!

Eliminate negativity when any part of your sport, business, or life suffers from your lack of intention or neglect. Avoid negative thoughts and statements when things don't meet your expectations.

The champion works on all parts of his or her life, business, or sport. The difference is they remain steadfast in holistically seeing the sum of their parts as the best. Weaknesses are not weaknesses. They are areas of growth. They are challenges that inspire the champion to think and act positively.

To combat the Teeter-Totter Effect™, extreme positivity must be in force. Have no thoughts of being a victim or a judge. It's the irate and disappointed judge in you that disrupts the playground with a mental sledgehammer to the low end of the teeter-totter.

Balance is the key to a successful life. Thought equilibrium will keep you at a high daily standard and from here, it's a short hop away to a peak performance Zone state.

Recently, a young golfer was riding the highs and lows of the Tee-ter-Totter Effect™. He pledged he would start selling himself on his own awesomeness. Five days and nights in a row his positive self-talk was exemplary. He was the poster guy for positive belief and expectancy. When a part of his game was down, he pictured it up. Relentless was his positivity! Results of 67-66-72 arrived and victory was his reward.

Escape from the positive-negative Teeter-Totter Effect™ and get on the high wire of peak performance. It's time to perform in the Zone.

CHAPTER 37

Be Decisive!

Now that The Blueprint has been created and your success pathway is set, decisiveness will be needed if you get lost or off track. These are decisions on how you will live your life.

Decisiveness, however, is missing in modern society. We fluctuate. We vacillate. We waver. We hem and haw (eastern Kentucky). We flip-flop. We procrastinate. We divert. We pivot. We drag it out. We put it off. We avoid the decision. We pass the buck. We conveniently delay because of indecision.

It's time to be bold in your life. It's time to become decisive!

General Life

▶ Now you know that "No" is the new yes. No is final. It is decisive. Say "No" to avoid putting off the answer. Use NO judicially as a tool to be decisive.

▶ Upgrade your greeting. The question of "How are you"? is asked dozens of times each day of your life. "I'm awesome!" or another strong greeting is the definitive response of a confident person. It is decisive in stating, "This is who I am!"

Wellness

"I am going to get in shape. I am finding a trainer and will get started," you blurt out to yourself and anyone that will listen. How many of us conveniently don't do it. Be decisive in getting started. Set the timeline. Be decisive in attending every training session, eating your agreed upon meal plan, and mentally acting as if you already have the body desired. "Do you want a donut? One's not going to hurt you," a co-worker states. **DO NOT EAT THAT DONUT.**

Parent

Say what you mean and mean what you say. Remember that your child is still in life training. How you deal with him or her will set a precedent for future discussions and your decisiveness or lack thereof could and probably will be passed on to your future grandchildren. "You're grounded! No cell phone for two weeks." Three days later (after your child has acted like Mother Teresa) you cave and give in. "Okay...you've been so good, we're going to give your phone back." **AVOID DOING**

THIS. Teach risk and reward. Stick to what you said or don't say it. Be decisive!

Relationship

You ask, "Do I look good in this tie?" You already know the answer. You just need validation. Be decisive in all facets of your relationship. Be strong-minded in deciding where to vacation, eat dinner, what to wear, or how to budget your finances. Add your confidence to the partnership and the union will become stronger.

Home

When negotiating with home improvement third parties, make it very clear about what you want. Document all conversations. Get estimates and firm quotes in writing. Assume nothing. Always stand your ground. NEVER pay full upfront (unless it's your thirty-year-old son doing the work and he desperately needs the cash). Pay a deposit. Pay the balance ONLY after a full inspection and you are 100 percent satisfied. Take charge. It's your home. Be decisive!

Other Family Members

This part of your life includes your interaction with siblings, aunts and uncles, cousins, parents, and grandparents. Although compromise is recommended with family members, be decisive with your feelings and actions. Tell it like it is with a positive win-win demeanor. Be firm on having only positive interactions. Do not allow negativity to enter your home. See what's best for these important relationships and be decisive in making it so.

Personal Finance:

What do you do with your money? Do you spend or save? How much and where do you invest? Who can help you? Do you have a long-term plan?

These questions need very specific answers to secure your future and improve or maintain your quality of life. This part of your life requires definite decisions. Weigh your options and research potential experts for your insurance, savings, estate planning, banking, and investment needs. **DO NOT** put this off! Be decisive and you'll sleep better at night.

Golf

"This looks like a six iron," you say out loud. Your caddie agrees. However, a little voice in the back of your mind whispers, "seven iron." What do you do? Know that intuition is real time information that your conscious mind does not possess. **HIT YOUR 7-IRON!** Period.

When you practice on the range, be decisive on exactly (hula-hoop sized targets) where you want the ball to go. Be decisive. See the line or shape of the shot as it heads to a specific landing spot. And with no more thought, let it fly.

Business

Successful businesses and careers are built on positive decision-making. Be decisive in your short and long-term goals. Be decisive with your brand personality. Be decisive with your strategies and tactics. Be upfront and direct with your team. Do not compromise your principles and values. Your customers and/or clients will positively react to decisive messaging and interactions.

Leadership

Great leaders are decisive. Bolstering confidence within your career, family, or community requires a leader to act the part. Walking into a meeting with a Zone mindset sets the tone for the meeting. Become the positive leader your business, career or family deserves and needs.

Most decisions in life can be made within 90-seconds of understanding the challenge. However, some decisions such as getting engaged or married, buying a new home, filing for divorce, moving to a new city, or changing careers, etc. may require gathering more information. Sleep on these life-altering decisions. Take your time. However, when you come to a conclusion, be decisive on the action required and **DO NOT** look back and second-guess yourself.

Good fortune favors the bold!

This statement becomes a mindset for most champions in life, business, and sports. If your life requires re-invention or re-direction, be decisive in your overall personal makeover.

BE DECISIVE!

Decisiveness is an important ingredient to becoming your authentic, genuine best self.

Decisively attract the Zone in all you do!

CHAPTER 38

The Vision Room

Part of the **Russian Dolls**™ concept is to weekly **Go To Higher Ground**™ and peruse The Blueprint, using it as a Vision Board. A literal Vision Room is a great place to physically house The Blueprint and picture your success.

Where do you physically plan the solutions for your life's challenges? Do you have a special room in your home where your visions, goals, and tasks are visually organized for you to readily see? Do you have a place at work where people can meet and exchange plans, ideas, and information in a proactive way? Does this workplace room have the company vision, goals, strategies, and tactics placed on the walls?

Governments, businesses, political parties, and NFL teams have private command centers. Here experts monitor and listen to the media and the public, respond to inquiries, evaluate pertinent data, and produce opinions to determine the best course of action. These command centers enable an organization to function as designed and perform day-to-day operations, regardless of what's happening around it.

This is a war room. Please rename this as you see fit. I call it **The Vision Room.**

Place all your personal and professional Visions, Big Rocks, Tasks, strategies, and tactics on the walls in a private room in your home or office (behind lock and key). If appropriate, place your clients' photos and their main Visions or Big Rocks on one of the walls.

In one client's private Vision Room, there are four walls, no windows, and one swivel chair positioned in the middle of the room. One wall is for everything that is Point B. This houses her destination. Another wall has Point A. This showcases the exact position she is in now. A third wall contains all of her clients. The fourth wall showcases all of the possible strategies and tactics for executing the daily tasks for advancing her life from A to B.

Seeing this room firsthand will let you know exactly what, how, and when this person will achieve her dreams. Why not you?

It is in this room that you proactively daydream. Regularly envision each Vision and Big Rock coming to fruition. This is your mental sanctuary for making things happen.

Equip your room with computers, printers, desk, peace and quiet, landline phone, scanner, television, fax machine, microphone, headset, and soundboard for recording, awesome tunes when desired, external hard drive, and pictures that motivate and inspire you.

The main function of this room is for planning, strategy, and tactics. And of course, it's for visualization. From the center of your room, you can sit in a swivel chair and peruse your life with total freedom. Here you can also manage your overall S.C.O.R.E.° Level or attitude.

It's within these walls that your thoughts are set free to wander, imagine, and create. Within this sanctuary you can envision your success.

Where do you escape? Do you have a Vision Room? I just learned that the LA Dodgers have a room where you can go and turn off the lights and visualize. I like that! In fact, in most sports arenas around the country, I've sequestered clients in a small room where their visualization takes place. They get alone in a private, dark room inside every sports arena and visualize with me on the phone or in person before games.

What is a Vision Board? Inside the Vision Room, create one wall for the major macro-items (Visions) to be accomplished in the future. This is your main Vision Board.

Seeing your life unfold in front of you gives you clarity. It's here that you can see what's missing, if anything. You can adjust and adapt to any and all ever-changing conditions, circumstances and situations. Here you can find peace and harmony. Change your thoughts and your emotions change. Change your emotions and your actions change. Change your actions and your life changes.

Think about what you think about. Once a week (possibly in your Vision Room) peruse The Blueprint and inspect ALL of your Life Arenas. Scour your past week for negative thoughts that may have occurred. Each Arena has thoughts about the past, future or present. Which Arena has the past that is lingering in your mind? Rid yourself of these damaging thoughts.

Which Arena needs your upmost attention and care? Which Visions and/or Big Rocks need revision, editing, or deleting? What resources, if any, do you need? Which of your Key People need to change or be deleted? Do you need to immunize yourself from their negative ways? Review the dynamic interaction of your Key People.

How is your Primary Arena? Are you on track to reach its Vision? What new strategies or tactics could be useful and effective?

Which Arena can use thought change? The accumulated thoughts of one Arena can be vast. With five people in one Arena that's potentially 10,000 or more thoughts collectively. Of course these thoughts are NOT about one Arena. However, the thoughts in each Arena must change in order for the Arena results to change.

In which Arena are you most positive? Which one holds your negative thoughts? Which Arena requires your aggressive attention?

While in your Vision Room, you can think and visualize in a proactive manner. You are mentally in control. It's time to think about what you think about. Change your thoughts in a positive way and you change your actions and consequently your positive results.

The non-champion has approximately 2,000 to 3,000 or more thoughts every day. The majority of these thoughts are in the future and the past. Most of these thoughts are in natural chaos. Regularly using the Vision Room can help reduce your extra, unnecessary thoughts.

Most champions think at least twenty-five percent less than non-champions. Their thoughts have little waste and are very well organized. To organize their thoughts, some use plain paper. Many use one wall of a room. A handful of them have a complete Vision Room. All have them organized in their mind. And the best of the best use everything available to them to prepare each performance and their next day, week, month, quarter, year, and life.

Champions win first then enter the arena. Non-champions enter the arena then try to figure out what to do.

Get prepared. Pay now in planning or pay later in worry, frustration, anguish, despair, anxiety, fear, and overall negative stress.

How do you live a simple, balanced, and abundant life? Build a personal and private Vision Room. Create your personal Vision Board. See it, as if it's so. See it, as it will be.

CHAPTER 39

A Life Worth Living

Now you have a well-thought out Blueprint for living, working, and playing. You can add or delete to this life design at any time. There are no rules for success.

Leaving your current comfort zone will allow you to expand your horizons, crush personal expectations, and turn your dreams into reality. Life is short. You know this. If I were personally coaching you, I would nudge you to venture further. Your goals would be accelerated. Why would I do this?

A life worth living is a life worth chasing its full potential.

Now is the time to review your completed Blueprint. Can it be bolstered or upgraded? You are now in possession of a powerful thought management system called S.C.O.R.E.° and it's never failed, although a few individuals have failed to use it. With S.C.O.R.E.° you have been provided concrete, proven 90-Second Rule™ tools, techniques, and tips for preparing, adjusting, and evaluating your daily performances.

Fear of failure is an illusion. It is not real. Fear of success is the same. Embrace "good fortune favors the bold" and your safety net will be removed and courage and confidence will be added. Embracing this motto removes the comfort zone shackles that trap us and it's freed thousands of individuals around the world to be their genuine, authentic best selves.

A life worth living places the vast majority of your thoughts in the moment. With seventy-five percent or more of your thoughts focused on the task at hand, your intuition will be primed to bolster your imagination and creativity. You now function more like a kid again, as well as any professional athlete locked in the Zone.

This mindset can be carried between Life Arenas. It can withstand the onslaught of S.C.O.R.E.° Breakers that bombard you. Present-tense living is living in the Zone.

Your dreams are real. They will manifest into reality. You can dictate the outcome with your Blueprint. Your newfound S.C.O.R.E.° lifestyle of peak performance is now your lifestyle. Use it wisely, share it where and when appropriate and bask in its glory.

CHAPTER 40

Jim's Final Thoughts

Do you have a Zone bucket list?

As you read this, I might be in the air traveling to beautiful Alaska or Tasmania. I may be climbing Machu Picchu in Peru, or walking in the El Yunque National Forest in northeastern Puerto Rico, the only tropical rain forest in the United States National Forest system, or having a glass of wine in a café on the streets of Prague. I may be looking over Lake Fannin writing my first novel. There is much to do and many places to go.

"Check this destination off my Zone bucket list" has been said many times in my life. How about you? What do you want to do that you haven't done? What new travel destination do you desire? What new experience do you want to have? What place or experience can get you in the Zone? These answers form your personal Zone bucket list and it needs to be sprinkled throughout your Blueprint.

There's only one rule for a successful life. There are no rules.

My mother, God rest her soul, always wanted to travel to France. "I can't wait to see Paris at night," she said with a faraway look in her eye. Paris was #1 on her bucket list. I've been there dozens of times and always shared my experiences with her. Finally, we made plans to travel to the City of Lights together. It would be an awesome Mom and son experience.

Unfortunately, her unexpected death nixed her top bucket list item. It was my only regret in life that I couldn't walk the Avenue des Champs-Élysees, visit the Arc de Triomphe, go to the top of the Eiffel Tower, take in the Louvre, and experience a glass of French wine in a quaint sidewalk café with my awesome mother.

Get busy on your personal bucket list. Know the bucket list of your family and closest friends.

In the scope of life, most people place themselves last in the "giving" department. Business owners pay themselves last as they scramble to meet payroll. Moms and dads sacrifice their own desires for their children. Work comes first and personal wellness comes last. All believe they'll eventually get around to it.

Make your bucket list. Schedule the timeline. Make the investment. Save for the major expenditures. Use this personal list as a reward for your hard work and efforts.

Some time ago, I met two self-made billionaires on the same day. I asked each the identical question. "What are the reasons for your success?" I was expecting a myriad of answers from luck, coincidence, hard work, perseverance, ingenuity, and timing to name a few. Both billionaires responded with "I reward myself." They each created a personal reward system for their achievements. Even though they could purchase anything they desired, they did not do it without reaching their self-imposed goals. Their bucket list was a reward system.

When was the last time you acknowledged and appreciated your work efforts? Tentatively book your reward in advance. When you reach your objective, collect your reward. Reach your weekly goals. Reward yourself. Reach your monthly goals. Reward yourself. Reach your annual goals. Attack your major bucket list.

Reward yourself for a job well done.

Incentives are uplifting, motivating and inspiring. Make your bucket list with this in mind. A few years ago, my wife had a personal project she was working on and I planned a surprise reward for her in advance. Knowing that she loved iconic Michael Jackson's music, I booked a round trip flight to London with tickets to see the King of Pop in person at his "This Is It!" concert in the O2 Arena. Obviously, this reward did not happen due to Michael's untimely death. Make your bucket list and help those you care about check off their personal list.

Life is short. No procrastination. Get in the Zone to reach your objectives. Reward yourself early and often for your accomplishments and remember the last letter in S.C.O.R.E.® is Enjoyment. Create your Zone bucket list and start checking off your rewards. And if you can facilitate another person's bucket list, their reward will give you everlasting pleasure and satisfaction. Get started.

By the time you are reading this book, I will be approaching seventy-years old or older. I have reinvented myself many times in my life. I call this the personal evolution of Jim. Change is an absolute and change is what all perennial champions in life do. Changing with the environment, adapting to new conditions, and adjusting to different circumstances and situations are all part of successful living.

My personal bucket list and a #$%&-it list have been made and I know what I want and DON'T want for the rest of my life. With "no rules for success" I will be taking up being a new grandparent, biking; painting, and learning Spanish. I have a few more books to write, too. I've never been to Maine and it's the only state in America I've missed. I'll enjoy fresh lobster when I finally get there. Why? Because I want to do it...that's all!

Please send me your results from reading *The Blueprint*. Act on this content. Keep me informed of your accomplishments and successes and drop me a note at askjim@jimfannin.com. You'll definitely put a Zone smile on my face.

My name is Jim Fannin. I coach champions. That's why I've been coaching you.

Be in the Zone!

Jim

My Life Blueprint

Arena:
Vision:
Due Date:
Big Rocks:
Tasks:
Key People:

My Life Blueprint

Arena:
Vision:
Due Date:
Big Rocks:
Tasks:
Key People:

My Life Blueprint

Arena:	
Vision:	
Due Date:	
Big Rocks:	
Tasks:	
Key People:	

My Life Blueprint

Arena:
Vision:
Due Date:
Big Rocks:
Tasks:
Key People:

My Life Blueprint

Arena:	
Vision:	
Due Date:	
Big Rocks:	
Tasks:	
Key People:	

My Life Blueprint

Arena:
Vision:
Due Date:
Big Rocks:
Tasks:
Key People:

My Life Blueprint

Arena:
Vision:
Due Date:
Big Rocks:
Tasks:
Key People:

My Life Blueprint

Arena:	
Vision:	
Due Date:	
Big Rocks:	
Tasks:	
Key People:	

My Life Blueprint

Arena:
Vision:
Due Date:
Big Rocks:
Tasks:
Key People:

Special Thanks

Mat Goggin: As one of my favorite, all-time clients, you placed The Blueprint name for this book in my mind years ago. More than an awesome professional golfer, you are a true champion in all ways.

Alice Patenaude/ Traci Shoblom: Thank you both for your superb editing and creative insight.

Robert Shook: You are not only one of the most accomplished and prolific nonfiction writers in America, but you are a great friend, mentor, and guide.

Jan Miller/Nena Oshman: You are literary agents extraordinaire.

David B. Stern: You rank as one of the top attorneys in your field in America. I appreciate your time and effort spent on this project.

Soren Thielemann: Your artistic views and creativity are unparalleled. Thank you for the book cover design.

Billie Brownell: As my editor at Post Hill Press, your candor and availability during this project was refreshing and needed.

Colby Sanford: You were one of my first Blueprint recipients over 33 years ago. As my daughter and mother to my first grandchild, you exceeded all my expectations.

CeCe Fannin: You stand and support all my creations and I appreciate you for a zillion reasons. Without your insight and encouragement, this book wouldn't have been written.

Acknowledgments

The sculpture on the front cover of *The Blueprint* is called *Self-Made Man*. It is the creation of accomplished sculptor **Bobbie Carlyle**. I am honored to have her original piece displayed prominently, as it depicts what this book is about. It showcases that "you control what you want your life to be." Go to bobbiecarlylesculpture.com to reach Ms. Carlyle.

The cover design is by acclaimed creative director **Soren Thielemann**, who can be reached at www.eatdanish.com.